Nebraska Pioneer Cookbook

Nebraska Pioneer Cookbook

Compiled by
Kay Graber

Illustrated by
Peggy W. Link

University of Nebraska Press
Lincoln and London

Publishers on the Plains
UNP

Copyright © 1974 by the University of Nebraska Press
All Rights Reserved

First Bison Book printing: October 1974

Most recent printing shown by first digit below:

5   6   7   8   9   10

Library of Congress Cataloging in Publication Data

Graber, Kay, 1938–   comp.
  Nebraska pioneer cookbook.

    1. Cookery, American—Nebraska. I. Title.
TX715.G723   641.5'9782   74–77089
ISBN 0–8032–5801–1
ISBN 0–8032–0945–2 cloth

Contents

Preface

IN ITS CUISINE as in its weather, Nebraska is a land of variety and extremes. Unlike other areas of the country—Boston with its baked beans and brown bread, the South with its spoon bread and chitlins—the state has no dishes invariably associated with it; its pioneers came relatively late in the parade of settlement, and they brought their recipes with them. Yet precisely because Nebraska cookery was imported—by settlers who might have originated anywhere between Peoria and Prague—it was remarkably cosmopolitan. (Even today, when nation-wide chains of fried chicken and hamburger stands have nearly obliterated regional distinctions, one can still find kolaches and roast duckling with sauerkraut in small-town Nebraska cafes.) Striking contrasts remained, side by side, well after the great tides of immigration of the 1870s and '80s. In 1893, the year in which historian Frederick Jackson Turner officially noted the end of the frontier—that "meeting point between savagery and civilization"—guests at a Lincoln reception for a famous actress dined on blue points on shell, fillet of beef aux truffles, and charlotte russe, while the occupants of dugouts a few miles from town most likely sat down to a supper of frontier fare like sowbelly and cornmeal mush.

Nebraska's pioneer food tells us much about how our

forebears lived, and in compiling this cookbook the aim has been to achieve a balance between recipes and descriptions of the way of life they exemplify. Although for the early period —through the territorial years—authentic contemporary recipes are relatively scarce (in a few cases, recipes from a somewhat later time were used in this section to illustrate typical foods), the problem for the later periods was one of choosing from an overabundance of recipes. The final selection had to be representative rather than comprehensive; recipes from the nineties alone could fill several cookbooks this size.

Inevitably, there were intriguing leads that proved impossible to follow up. In her Nebraska novel *My Ántonia*, Willa Cather alludes to the Bohemian custom of cooking cucumbers in milk and speaks of gathering blossoms for elderblow wine, but efforts to find recipes for either of these were unsuccessful. Professor Bernice Slote, who grew up in the Dutch communities of Firth and Hickman, says that her mother used to make elderblossom fritters, but the exact directions, if they were ever written down, have been lost. The further one delves into the subject of early-day food, the more examples of this sort that crop up: what, for instance, was the rough and ready served at the Herndon House in Omaha on Christmas Day, 1862?

Nineteenth-century housewives generally cooked by taste and touch rather than by formula. Although comprehensive printed cookbooks with detailed instructions had long been available and were published in sizable numbers in the late eighties and the nineties, it was possible to be an excellent cook without ever having recourse to one; consequently, recipes of the period are often lacking in specifics. A table of equivalents follows on the next page to aid in translating measurements into modern terms. Because of differences in stoves and variations in the quality of the ingredients used (the coarseness of the flour, the size of the eggs, etc.), these recipes should be taken more as general guides to be moderated by the cook's judgment and experience, than as precise blueprints.

Table of Equivalents

Weights and Measures

A speck equals one-quarter saltspoon.

Four saltspoons equal one teaspoon.

Three teaspoons equal one tablespoon.

Sixteen level tablespoons equal one cup (teacup or cof-feecup).

One cup equals eight ounces.

Four tablespoons equal one wineglass.

Two wineglasses equal one gill.

Two gills equal one cup.

Two cups equal one pint.

Two pints equal one quart.

One quart of flour makes one pound.

One pint of sugar makes one pound.

One heaping tablespoonful of flour or sugar makes one ounce.

One pint of soft butter makes one pound.

One pint of finely chopped meat, packed, makes one pound.

Ten average-sized eggs make one pound.

Oven Temperatures

Very slow:	225–250°	Moderately hot:	375°
Slow:	275–300°	Hot:	400–425°
Moderately slow:	325°	Very hot:	450°
Moderate:	350°		

The Early Days

ALTHOUGH the future state of Nebraska would appear on nineteenth-century maps as part of the "Great American Desert," its first inhabitants, various groups of Plains Indians, found it a veritable natural grocery store. For generations they lived on its wild game—especially bison, the mainstay of prairie life—and wild fruits and vegetables, supplemented by cultivated corn, beans, pumpkins, and squash. In 1804, William Clark and Meriwether Lewis, the first official representatives of the United States government to enter present Nebraska, inventoried its edible resources. A partial tally includes "deer, turkies, and grouse," elk, geese, ducks, plover, buffalo, white catfish as well as a variety of other fish, "an abundance of grapes," plums of three kinds, "two species of wild-cherries," hazelnuts, gooseberries, and "an excellent fruit, resembling a red currant, growing on a shrub like the privy, and about the height of the wild plum."

Jerky, dried meat preserved with salt obtained from natural deposits like those at the site of future Lincoln, and pemmican, which has been described as an early-day K-ration, were two of the most common foods of the nomadic tribes. Both were easily carried and kept well for months. If Indian cooks had had recipe books, the instructions for their preparation might have read like this.

JERKY

Cut bison or venison in foot-long strips, with the grain so it will be stringy, using any cut you can get strips from—rump, legs, etc. Prepare a very strong salt and water brine and dip the strips in it until the meat is white. Hang strips in the sun until thoroughly dry, and store in a ventilated container so that air can get to them. May be eaten dry or rehydrated. When stewed, jerky is very similar to fresh meat.

PEMMICAN

Combine equal parts of buffalo suet; dried fruit such as cherries, berries, and plums; and dried venison or other game. Add salt if available, and pound the mixture in a bowl or a hollow rock; then form into bricks. Dry in the sun, or near the fire in rainy weather. Pemmican may be eaten as is, by biting off chunks, or bricks may be simmered in water to make a thick soup or stew.

Like the Indians, early white explorers, traders, and missionaries lived largely off the land, carrying only as much of the basic items like flour, sugar, and coffee as their packs could accommodate. Even these were not in their present convenient form. Until the last decades of the nineteenth century, refined white sugar was scarce and expensive on the frontier; and when it was available, it was supplied in the form of loaves, or cubes. Brown sugar, much coarser than that we see today, was used extensively, as well as molasses. The flour, unbleached and perhaps unbolted, was subject to an unpleasant rawness (some recipes of the period instruct the cook to dry the flour in front of the fire before using it). Only green coffee was sold, and it had to be roasted and ground before brewing. Salt pork was a frontier staple because it kept almost indefinitely and was easily prepared: after soaking a few hours or over night in fresh water to remove the salt, it was generally fried.

When Fort Atkinson was established in 1820 near present Fort Calhoun as the westernmost outpost of the United States, the regulation daily ration called for three-fourths of a pound of pork or bacon, or one and one-fourth pounds of fresh or salted beef; eighteen ounces of bread or flour, or twelve ounces of hard bread, or one and one-fourth pounds of cornmeal; and one gill of whiskey per man. Two quarts of salt, four quarts of vinegar, and twelve quarts of peas or beans were allotted with every hundred rations. The War Department, apparently influenced by current medical theories, directed that meats were to be "boiled with a view to soup, sometimes roasted or baked, never fried," but from all evidence these eccentric instructions were generally ignored.

Although Fort Atkinson was abandoned after only seven years, agriculturally it was a great success. The abundant crops of corn, beets, cabbages, radishes, parsnips, carrots, and other vegetables, planted in an attempt to see if the post could be made self-sufficient, provoked one military inspector in the mid-1820s to complain irately that "the present system is destroying military spirit and making officers the base overseers of a troop of awkward ploughmen." Along with the hogs and cattle which were also raised at the fort, these provisions were augmented by wild game and wild berries and fruits in season.

WILD RABBIT

After cleaning the rabbit, wash it in cold water and hang up to freeze in order to loosen the meat fibers. Soak for a short time in salt water before cooking, to draw out the blood. Cut into pieces, washing each in cold water. Then put pieces in a stew pan filled with water in which a pinch of soda has been dissolved. Bring to a simmer, remove from the heat, and pour off the water. Put pieces back in the pan, add more water, and stew until the meat is loosened from the bone but not shredded. Then drain, add a little bacon fat, and fry the pieces brown; or bake them for about half an hour. Wild rabbit is best in the fall and winter months.

Beginning in the 1840s, the Platte River route became a major highway for travelers to Oregon and California. One of the first large groups of emigrants to follow that road were the Mormons who spent the winter of 1846–47 at Winter Quarters, now part of north Omaha, in their exodus to the Great Salt Lake. The Mormon women were notable for their resourcefulness, according to a contemporary observer.

They could hardly be called housewives in etymological strictness; but it was plain that they had once been such, and most distinguished ones. Their art availed them in their changed affairs. With almost their entire culinary material limited to the milk of their cows, some store of meal or flour, and a very few condiments, they brought their thousand and one receipts into play with a success that outdid for their families the miracle of the Hebrew widow's cruse. They learned to make butter on a march by the dashing of the wagon, and so nicely to calculate the working of barm in the jolting heats that, as soon after the halt as an oven could be dug in the hillside and heated, their well-kneaded loaf was ready for baking, and produced good leavened bread for supper.

Yeast bread was made by the sponge method, and the "barm"—yeast or starter—might or might not contain commercial yeast powders or compressed yeast.

GOOD YEAST

Boil one pound good flour, a quarter of a pound of moist [lump or New Orleans] sugar, and half an ounce of salt in two gallons of water for an hour. When nearly cold, bottle and cork it closely. It will be fit for use in twenty-four hours, and one pint will make eighteen pounds of bread.

YEAST MADE WITH PREPARED YEAST

Boil one dozen large potatoes, mash fine, and boil one quart of hops. When done, put the hop water and the mashed potatoes in the potato water. For one gallon, take one cup of sugar and one cup of salt; when cool, add yeast sufficient to have it get light. Keep in a warm place for two days, then put in a tight jar. For three or four loaves of bread take half a pint of the yeast, after stirring it up well.

YEAST BREAD

Sift the flour into a large bread pan or bowl; make a hole in the middle of it and pour in the yeast in the ratio of a half a teacupful of yeast to two quarts of flour; stir the yeast lightly; then pour in your "wetting," either milk or water, as you choose. If you use water, dissolve in it a bit of butter the size of an egg; if you use milk, no butter is necessary, but the milk must be scalded and cooled before it is added. Stir the "wetting" very lightly, but do not mix all the flour into it; then cover the pan with a thick blanket or towel and set it in a warm place to rise (this is called "putting the bread in sponge"). When the sponge is light, add a teaspoonful of salt and mix all the flour in the pan with the sponge, kneading it well; then let it stand two hours or more until it has risen quite light. Knead it again until the dough is elastic, then form into loaves, place in baking tins, and allow to rise until the bulk is doubled. Bake in a quick oven from forty-five to sixty minutes (the temperature is right when a tablespoonful of flour browns in five minutes).

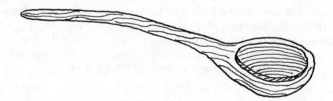

Mid-nineteenth-century scientists were sharply divided over the comparative nutritional value of yeast bread and bread raised with saleratus—potassium bicarbonate or sodium bicarbonate (baking soda). Proponents of yeast bread, while admitting that stale yeast or overfermentation produced a sour, unpalatable product, contended that "saleratus and soda in our bread have more to do with the thin bones, rotten teeth and flabby looks of our children—large and small—than many would imagine." Supporters of the opposite position, on the other hand, argued that "a large proportion of the bread in some communities, is scarcely more than an active form of yeast, thrown into the stomach only to produce fermentation and a host of disorders. And then we witness, of course, the blue vapors, which under different aspects, are as ruinous to the welfare and peace of a family as are those of a distillery." In all seriousness this group recommended making bread with weak muriatic (hydrochloric) acid and baking soda.

UNFERMENTED BREAD

Take of flour three pounds, bicarbonate of soda nine drachms, hydrochloric acid, eleven, specific gravity 1 16/100. About 25 oz. of water will be required to form the dough. First mix the soda and flour as thoroughly as possible. This is best done by shaking the soda (in fine powder) from a sieve over the flour with one hand, while the flour is stirred with the other, and then passing the mixture once or more through the sieve. Next pour the acid into the water, and diffuse it by stirring them well together, avoiding the use of any metallic utensil that the acid might come in contact with. Then mix the flour and water so prepared as speedily as possible. The dough should be put into a quick oven speedily. This manner of making bread will, if practiced, be found to be a great improvement, and advantageous compared with the fermenting method, and also the quality will be found vastly superior to the antique "leavened bread."

By the early 1850s, tens of thousands of goldseekers—"Argonauts," as they were called—had thronged the Platte River road on their way to California. The heavy traffic brought permanent settlers, and by the time Nebraska Territory was officially organized in 1854 the area claimed some 2,700 citizens. At Bellevue, Peter Sarpy, whose trading post was the center of the oldest permanent settlement in the territory, advertised a wide variety of foodstuffs for sale: "Crushed, clarified, loaf and brown sugar, molasses, syrup molasses, golden syrup, superior tea, Rio and Java coffee, sassafras, ginger, nutmegs, . . . vinegar, pickles, pepper sauce." Caroline Morton, wife of the young politician and editor J. Sterling Morton who is now best remembered as the founder of Arbor Day, confirmed the availability of supplies at Bellevue: "There is plenty of good beef, venison, and wild game, vegetables of all kinds, and two or three stores where they keep all kinds of eatables, drinkables and wearables—even oysters put up in cans, pickles and preserves can be procured." Most early Nebraskans lacked the conveniences of a well-stocked store, however, and their diet was definitely pioneer fare: according to historian Everett Dick, the midnight supper served at the inaugural ball for Territorial Governor Mark W. Izard in early 1855 consisted of "coffee with brown sugar, peculiar sandwiches made of thick slices of bread and bacon, and dried apple pie."

DRIED APPLE PIE

Wash the fruit thoroughly, soak over night in water enough to cover. In the morning, stew slowly, until nearly done, in the same water. Sweeten to taste. The crust, both upper and under, should be rolled thin; a thick crust to a fruit pie is undesirable.

While dried apples were a common item of frontier food, many found them unappetizing—dirty and tough. Their sentiments were expressed in a ditty:

> Spit in my ears
> And tell me lies,
> But give me no
> Dried apple pies.

Other fruits and vegetables—peaches, corn, pumpkins, squash, string beans, even rhubarb—were also preserved by drying. The Nebraska Writers' Project pamphlet "Early Nebraska Cooking" recounts the adventures of one neophyte in drying apples and corn:

> A young farm girl, named Luella, "hired out" to a neighboring housewife. . . . Luella, who was a newcomer to Nebraska, did not

understand all of the frontier customs, so every once in a while she made some strange mistakes. The most humorous of these occurred one afternoon when the lady of the house made preparations for drying corn and apples.

The apple drying was simple, as all it required was a sharp knife with which to peel the fruit, after which the apples were sliced in round rings, threaded and hung in the sun to dry. The housewife was called away to see a sick neighbor before Luella came to the corn. Luella, left alone, started in with the corn in the very way she had the apples. She cut the kernels off the cobs, then began stringing them.

Impatience could not have been one of Luella's faults, or tedious work a boredom. Because, during the course of the afternoon, she strung corn until all of the cotton thread was exhausted, after which she used spools of silk sewing thread.

The housewife, upon her return near suppertime, stood speechless when she saw the bizarre effects created by the lines of gay-colored thread which carried their burdens of sweet corn kernels. Needless to say, Luella finished her education on corn drying by using a lean-to roof and some mosquito netting.

When sugar was available, "leathers" were a favorite way of preserving peaches and other fruits.

PEACH LEATHER

Measure one-half cupful of sugar for each pound of peeled, stoned peaches. Put fruit and sugar into a preserving kettle, bring slowly to a boil, and simmer until most of the moisture has cooked away, mashing to a smooth paste as they cook. Oil a large china platter, cover with a piece of muslin, and spread the cooked peaches on it in a thin layer. Put the paste in the sun till thoroughly dry, then roll it in the cloth and store in a cool, dry place. To eat, unroll and tear off pieces.

Tomatoes were packed in a brine, and wild plums were commonly preserved without sweetening in the vinegar formed by their own juices.

TO PRESERVE WILD PLUMS

Gather plums when fully ripe, put in barrels, jars, tubs, or anything that will hold water; cover them with water after filling up. There forms a scum on the top which keeps them from the air. They need no careful sealing, or anything but a safe place from freezing during the winter, although it is advisable to weight down the lid.

Along with sugar, other basic commodities were often scarce, too. Until a settler could plant a garden and acquire livestock, he might have to do without eggs, milk, butter, or lard. Eighteen-year-old Mollie Dorsey, who moved with her family from Indiana to a claim near Nebraska City in 1857, left a description of a summer Sunday dinner which she improvised for unexpected guests:

We had about run ashore for provision, not having had an installment since we moved. Having no milk, no butter, eggs, nor vegetables, it seemed a gloomy prospect, for those that wished to be hospitable. Mother, who feels our circumstances more keenly with her proud English spirit, took the babies and fled to her retreat in the woods, where she often goes to gain her equilibrium. I knew our bachelor friends would expect a square meal, so as I'm chief cook anyway, I knew the honors devolved upon me, so put my wits to work accordingly. We have put up a brush kitchen at the end of the house, as it grew so hot we could not cook indoors, so leaving the girls to entertain the gentlemen, . . . I started my fire and began to think up my bill of fare. I had a few days before found a large bush of wild gooseberries, almost large enough for use. The boys soon gathered them and . . . they were soon picked over. I had no lard, so fried out some fat meat, made some pie crust and baked a pie. Then made a cake using my shortening, and vinegar and saleratus to make it light, took my dry bread and dipped it in batter and fried it nice and brown, floured and fried my fat meat, had a good cup of coffee, and a dish of stewed gooseberries.

In the meantime the girls had set the table in our best appointments, with a snowy linen cloth, nice glassware, and our handsome dishes, and when all was ready, they hunted up Mother, and when she came in she looked surprised enough, but I, as cool as a cucumber as tho we were accustomed to such a "spread." The men ate with a relish that corresponded with their verdict, that "it was the best meal they had had in the country."

Mollie didn't fare so well in the home of a family of southerners while "boarding around" as a schoolteacher:

Their manner of living is so different from ours that it just about used me up. For breakfast we had corn bread, salt pork, and black coffee. For dinner, greens, wild ones at that, boiled pork, and cold corn bread, washed down with "beverage." For supper we had hoe cake, cold greens, and pork with coffee. The "beverage" was put upon the table in a wooden pail and dished out in tin cups. When asked if I would have some of the "aforesaid," I said "yes," thinking it perhaps was cider, but found out it was vinegar and brown sugar and warm creek water.

From the establishment of the first settlements until after the turn of the century, cornmeal was a major item of diet in Nebraska. Because corn was easily grown, the meal was used almost to the exclusion of wheat flour by many frontier families, and even the cobs were utilized for fuel in the combination cooking and heating stoves. After the mature corn was ground at the local mill, the cook sifted out the hulls with a wood-rimmed shaker sieve. Attempts were made to vary the ways in which it was prepared, but as one old-timer remarked, no matter how you tried to disguise it, it was still corn.

An article in an 1861 issue of the *Nebraska Farmer* arguing the superiority of corn over wheat and potatoes gave thirty-three recipes for its use. Here are some of them.

HASTY PUDDING, OR "MUSH"

We place this first as the most common and most easily made. No one ever "took sick" from eating mush and milk, or fried mush in any suitable quantity. (We knew a student well, who left the active labors of the farm to pursue his studies in an Academy. The first term he used a variety of food, and was in poor health. The next term of 11 weeks he ate *only* mush and milk, for breakfast, dinner, and supper, and actually grew fat on it, while he lost all headache, and though pursuing five heavy studies, he was first in his class, and went through the term strong and vigorous, without an hour of lost time, though he worked enough in the field and garden, at 8 cents an hour, to pay all his expenses.) "Mush and milk" is seldom relished, because few people know how to make the mush. The whole secret is in cooking it thoroughly. Rightly made it is not "*hasty* pudding." A well made "mush" is one that has boiled not less than a full hour. Two hours are better. The meal needs to be cooked; then it is both good and palatable. The rule is: Mix it very thin and boil it down, avoiding any burning or scorching, and salt it just right to suit the general taste. Prepare a good kettle full for supper, to be eaten with milk, sugar, molasses, syrup, or sweetened cream, or sweetened milk. If a good supply be left to cook, and be cut in slices and fried well in the morning, the plate of wheaten bread will be little in demand. It must be fried well, not crisped, or burned, or soaked in fat. If thoroughly soaked through in the kettle, it will only need to be heated through on the griddle. If not cooked well in the kettle, longer frying will be necessary.

DRY MUSH AND MILK

Parch corn quite brown, grind it in a clean coffee mill or pound it in a mortar, and let it soak in warm milk until softened; then if too thick add more milk and eat when cold. Or meal may be browned and eaten in the same manner.

SAMP

This is a good method of using corn, and a popular one when well tried—made not of the white hominy of various grades of coarseness and sold in small bags in various stages of freshness; but yellow corn fresh plucked from the fields, or well preserved, and but recently *crushed* (not ground) at the village mill. Boiled well, as directed above for pudding, no dish is more popular than this with children, and many grown people, particularly in Autumn and Winter. It can be used with syrup, or good milk, or sugar, or both. Like hasty pudding, it is good for the second day. The various grades of "hominy" are very good articles of food but not so good as samp.

BOILED INDIAN CORN (RIPE)

Take common yellow corn, and boil it in a weak lye, until the hulls are broken and easily slip off. Then pour off the lye and wrinse the corn thoroughly. Boil it until soft, in clear water, adding a little salt. Eat with cream and sugar or butter and syrup, or simply with butter as a vegetable.

AN EXCELLENT CORN CAKE

Take one pint of corn meal, one quart of sour milk, four eggs well beaten, two tablespoonfuls of sugar, and soda enough to sweeten the milk. Mix well together, and bake in pans. To have any corn cake with eggs light, the eggs must be well beaten. (For this recipe the sum of $3 was originally paid—to a baker we suppose.)

JOHNNY CAKE, OR CORN BREAD

The following (not before published) we formerly copied from the MS. of a good housewife in Georgia. Beat two eggs very light, mix with them, alternately, one pint of sour milk or butter milk, and one pint of meal. Add one tablespoon of melted butter. Dissolve one tablespoonful of soda in a little of the milk and add to the mixture. Last but not least, beat hard together and bake quick.

FLORIDA JOHNNY CAKE

The following simple recipe we picked up in Florida, and know by experience that it makes good bread: Take one tumbler of milk, one of Indian meal, beat up one egg, mix in the whole together and bake well.

VIRGINIA CORN DODGERS

Take three pints of unsifted yellow corn meal, one tablespoonful of lard, and one pint of milk. Work all well together, and bake in cakes the size of the hand, and an inch thick. We have often eaten this in Dixie's land, and know it to be palatable—to a hungry man highly so.

YEAST CORN BREAD

Three pints of meal, and one of rye or Graham flour, two tablespoonfuls of sugar and one teaspoonful of salt. One yeast cake softened in warm water. This should be mixed with warm water to a dough just compact enough not to run, and then be put in a deep pan, and left by the fire until it rises about one fourth higher than when mixed. Bake in a moderate oven five hours. This makes a thick crust upon the top which is to be lifted off, and the remainder eaten warm. Slice and heat in a steamer for breakfast. The crusts are to be softened in warm water, and crumbled fine for the wetting of the next loaf, and the cook will be surprised to find the second experiment far superior to the first.

RYE AND INDIAN LOAVES

(First rate—the real Yankee loaf.) Scald two quarts of Indian meal, and when cold add one quart unbolted rye flour, three-quarters of a pint molasses, one tablespoon salt, and water enough to make a stiff sponge or batter. Pour into deep iron pots or kettles, and bake in a slow oven for three or four hours. If in a brick oven, leave it over night. A standard bread in New England, eaten both hot and cold.

APPLE CORN BREAD

Mix one pint of Indian meal with one pint of sweet milk, and add one quart of chopped sweet apples, and a small teaspoonful of salt. Bake in shallow pans in a quick oven. To be eaten hot.

PUMPKIN INDIAN LOAF

Scald one quart of Indian meal, and stir in one pint stewed pumpkin, mashed fine, or sifted; add one teaspoonful salt, one-quarter pint molasses, mixing to a stiff batter. Bake in deep iron dishes as rye and Indian loaves, above.

"WHITPOT" (INDIAN)

Take one quart of sweet milk, one-half pint of Indian meal, two or three eggs, one-half teaspoonful of salt, and four tablespoonfuls of sugar. Boil one pint of the milk, stir in the meal while boiling, cook five minutes, and add the remainder of the milk. Beat the sugar and eggs together, and when cold stir the whole thoroughly, and bake one hour in a deep dish. To be eaten either hot or cold.

MOLASSES OR MOCK WHITPOT

Indian meal and milk same as above, adding one-quarter pint of molasses, and cooking in the same manner. A very cheap and good pudding, easily made.

INDIAN DUMPLING

Scald one pint Indian meal, one small tablespoonful of shortening, one-quarter teaspoonful salt, one-quarter teaspoonful soda or saleratus. Boil one hour in a bag. Serve hot, with gravy and meats.

YEAST CORN MUFFINS

One quart of Indian meal, a heaping spoonful of butter, one quart of milk, a salt spoon of salt, two tablespoonfuls of yeast, and one of molasses. Let it rise four or five hours. Bake in rings. It may also be baked in shallow pans. Bake one hour.

CORN GRIDDLE CAKE

Take one quart of sour milk, three eggs, one large teaspoonful of saleratus, one small teaspoonful of salt, and add sufficient meal and flour to cause them to turn easily on the griddle. Use a third as much flour as meal.

BAKED INDIAN PUDDING

Boil one pint of sweet milk, stir in one cup of meal while boiling, pour into a baking dish and add one-half cup of molasses, two tablespoonfuls of sugar, one teaspoonful of ginger, one-half teaspoonful of salt, and a little nutmeg. Then add one pint of sweet milk with one egg well beaten. Put into the oven and bake one hour.

BOILED INDIAN PUDDING

Three pints of milk; ten tablespoonfuls of sifted Indian meal, half a cup of molasses, and two eggs. Scald the meal with the milk, add the molasses and a spoonful of salt. Put in the eggs when it is cold enough not to scald them. Stir in a tablespoonful of ginger. Put it into a bag and tie so that it will be about two-thirds full of the pudding, in order to give room to swell. The longer it is boiled, the better. Some like a little chopped suet added.

MAIZE GRUEL FOR INVALIDS

Stir in a large tablespoonful of Indian meal into a teacupful of cold water, and salt. Have ready a quart of cold water in a spider, pour in the mixture, and boil it gently twenty minutes, stirring it constantly the last five. To make it richer boil raisins in the gruel, and sugar, nutmeg, and a little butter.

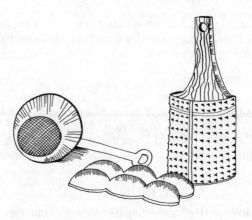

Other recipes from the territorial period show how the early Nebraskans made do, and what they had to make do with.

TO MAKE A CAKE WITHOUT BUTTER

Take a piece of salt pork, and melt it down, and strain it through a piece of muslin. Set it aside until cool. It is then white and firm, and may be used like butter in any kind of cake.

TO MAKE SUGAR OF SORGHUM

Boil sorghum thick, draw off in open coolers, and place in a warm room, say 82 degrees Fahrenheit, and in about ten days it will be sufficiently granulated. Then place it into barrels or funnel shaped boxes with perforated bottoms, and allow it to stand in a warm room to drain off the molasses, and in a short time you will have sugar for use.

A GOOD RECEIPT FOR VINEGAR

Take forty gallons of water, one gallon of molasses, and four pounds of acetic acid. It will be fit for use in a few days. Acetic acid costs but twenty five cents a pound. This is the receipt by which most of the cider vinegar is made which is sold in the country stores.

Nebraska Pioneer Cookbook

PICKLED PLUMS

To pickle seven pounds of plums, take four and a half of sugar, one quart of vinegar, four ounces of cinnamon, two ounces of cloves, put the spices in a bag, scald the sugar, spice and vinegar together, then pour over the plums, cover tight, let them stand on the stove and keep hot, not boil, for four hours.

PICKLED CABBAGE

Slice the cabbage and boil ten minutes, then drain and pack in the jar. To one gallon of vinegar add one teacup of molasses, and spice and pepper to suit the taste, and heat and pour upon the cabbage.

TOMATO CHOWDER

Take green tomatoes, cut a small piece off the stem end, and also from the other side; then lay them in a pan. Sprinkle with salt, pour boiling water on them, and let them stand ten minutes. Chop them up fine, putting in some cabbage, horse radish, and peppers; and vinegar on, and they are ready to pack in crocks. They make an excellent dish to serve with meat. Try it.

TOMATO CATSUP

To half a bushel of skinned tomatoes, add one quart of good vinegar, one pound of salt, a quarter of a pound of black pepper, two ounces of African cayenne, a quarter of a pound of allspice, six good onions, one ounce of cloves, and two pounds of brown sugar. Boil this mass for three hours, constantly stirring it to keep it from burning. When cool strain it through a sieve.

BAKED TOMATOES

Tomatoes baked the same as apples, and eaten with salt, pepper and butter, are excellent. Also eaten with sugar and cream.

RHUBARB SYRUP

Cut rhubarb into small pieces, simmer it over a slow fire one hour, with a very little water; or it may be baked in a jar; then strain it and add sugar to the palate. When it is young it is, like apples, unnecessary to be peeled. If sweetened with the best of sugars (loaf is best), it will, if preserved air tight, and set in a cool place, keep good for many months, and will be found to be pleasant and refreshing at all times and seasons.

ELDERBERRY WINE

To make this wine, take one quart of the juice of the ripe berries, and add two quarts of water, and three and one-half pounds of sugar. When the sugar is dissolved, strain and put in two tablespoonfuls of yeast to each gallon of the liquid, letting it stand about fifteen days in open vessels, after which drain off and bottle. Keep in a cool place.

TOMATO WINE

To make tomato wine, take small, ripe tomatoes, pick off the stems, put them into a basket or tub, wash clean, then mash well, and strain through a linen rag (a bushel will make five gallons, pure), then add two and a half or three pounds of good brown sugar to each gallon; then put into a cask, and ferment and fine, as for raspberry wine. If two gallons of water be added to each bushel of tomatoes the wine will be as good.

GOOSE BOILED WITH ONION SAUCE

When your goose is nicely prepared, singe it and pour over it a quart of boiling milk; let it stand in the milk all night, then take it out and dry it exceedingly well with a cloth, season it with pepper and salt, chop an onion and some sage, put them into your goose, sew it up at the neck until the next day; then put it in a pan of cold water, cover it close, and let it boil slowly one hour. Serve it with onion sauce.

By 1860 stage coach service had been established across Nebraska. The Concord stages, accommodating up to nine passengers, made the jolting run at an average of five to six miles an hour, with meal stops at stations located at about thirty-mile intervals along the route. The famous English explorer Sir Richard Burton, who took the stage trip across the plains to California in 1860, left a lively account incorporating his impressions—mostly negative—of the food. At Plum Creek station, near present Lexington, he dined on buffalo—"Probably bull beef," he wrote,

> the worst and driest meat, save elk, that I have ever tasted; indeed, without the assistance of pork fat, we found it hard to swallow. As every one knows, however, the two-year-old cow is the best eating, and at this season the herds are ever in the worst condition. The animals calve in May and June, consequently they are in August completely out of flesh. They are fattest about Christmas, when they find it difficult to run. All agree in declaring that there is no better meat than that of the young buffalo; the assertion, however, must be taken *cum grano salis*. Wild flesh was never known to be equal to tame, and that monarch did at least one wise thing who made the loin of beef Sir Loin. The voyageurs and travellers who cry up the buffalo as so delicious, have been living for weeks on rusty bacon and lean antelope; a rich hump with its proper menstruum, a cup of *café noir* as strong as possible, must truly be a "tit bit." They boast that the fat does not disagree with the eater; neither do three pounds of heavy pork with the English ploughboy, who has probably taken less exercise than the Canadian hunter. Before long, buffalo flesh will reach New York, where I predict it will be held as inferior to butcher's meat as is the antelope to park-fed venison.

Burton's prediction was only partially accurate: buffalo tongue was relished as a delicacy in the East, and professional hunters slaughtered the animals en masse for the tongues, humps, and hides, leaving the remainder of the carcasses to rot. Within twenty years the great herds were almost extinct.

British visitors, who came in numbers to see the American West after the Civil War, and particularly after the completion of the transcontinental railroad, generally agreed with the substance of Burton's assessment of western food. At a station near the present Nebraska-Wyoming border he observed:

The Early Days 19

Nebraska Pioneer Cookbook

Our breakfast was prepared in the usual prairie style. First the coffee—three parts burnt beans—which had been duly ground to a fine powder and exposed to the air, lest the aroma should prove too strong for us, was placed on the stove to simmer till every noxious principle was duly extracted from it. Then the rusty bacon, cut into thick slices, was thrown into the fry-pan; here the gridiron is unknown, and if known would be little appreciated, because it wastes the "drippings," which form with the staff of life a luxurious sop. Thirdly, antelope steak, cut off a corpse suspended for the benefit of flies outside, was placed to stew within influence of the bacon's aroma. Lastly came the bread, which of course should have been "cooked" first. The meal is kneaded with water and a pinch of salt; the raising is done by means of a little sour milk, or more generally by the deleterious yeast-powders of the trade. The carbonic acid gas evolved by the addition of water must be corrected and the dough must be expanded by saleratus or prepared carbonate of soda or alkali, and other vile stuff, which communicates to the food the green-yellow tinge, and suggests many of the properties of poison. A hundred-fold better, the unpretending chapati, flap-jack, scone, or, as the Mexicans prettily called it, "tortilla"! The dough after being sufficiently manipulated upon a long, narrow smooth board is divided into "biscuits" and "dough nuts," and finally it is placed to be half cooked under the immediate influence of the rusty bacon and graveolent antelope. "Uncle Sam's stove," be it said with every reverence for the honoured name it bears, is a triumph of convenience, cheapness, unwholesomeness and nastiness—excuse the word, nice reader. This travellers' bane has exterminated the spit and gridiron, and makes everything taste like its neighbour: by virtue of it, mutton borrows the flavour of salmon-trout, tomatoes resolve themselves into greens.—I shall lose my temper if the subject is not dropped.

The adulteration of coffee to make it go further and the use of ersatz preparations were common frontier practices, for coffee was scarce and expensive. In addition to beans, substitutes were made from cornmeal and sorghum, mixed to a gummy dough and baked until brown; dried peas; and parched corn, barley, rye, or wheat. A correspondent to the *Nebraska Farmer* recommended carrots and okra:

CARROT COFFEE

Wash and slice the carrots across in pieces half an inch thick, and dry in the sun or oven so as not to cook them. When dry, brown and use the same as coffee. Prepared in this manner, equal parts of carrots and coffee is an excellent substitute for the genuine Rio.

OKRA OR GUMBO COFFEE

This makes the best coffee of any article that I have ever used as a substitute for coffee. The seed should be browned the same as coffee and makes a very palatable drink alone, but is a little better if a little coffee is used with it. The plant is very productive and is easily grown. An ounce of the seed will produce enough for almost any family. The seed can be procured of any seedsman for 25 to 30 cents per ounce.

Travelers on the eastern border of Nebraska Territory began to find some of the refinements of civilization by the early 1860s. For Christmas dinner, 1862, the Herndon House, a well-known Omaha hostelry, offered a menu which included, along with the standard frontier foods, such treats as salmon, oysters, and lobster.

OYSTER SOUP

Two quarts of oysters, one teacupful of hot water, one quart milk, two tablespoonfuls butter, salt and pepper. Strain all the liquor from the oyster; add the water, and heat. When near the boil, add the seasoning, then the oysters. Cook about five minutes from the time they begin to simmer, until they ruffle. Stir in the butter, cook one minute, and pour into the tureen. Stir in the boiling milk.

ROAST TURKEY

Select a young turkey; remove all the feathers carefully, singe it over a burning newspaper on the top of the stove;

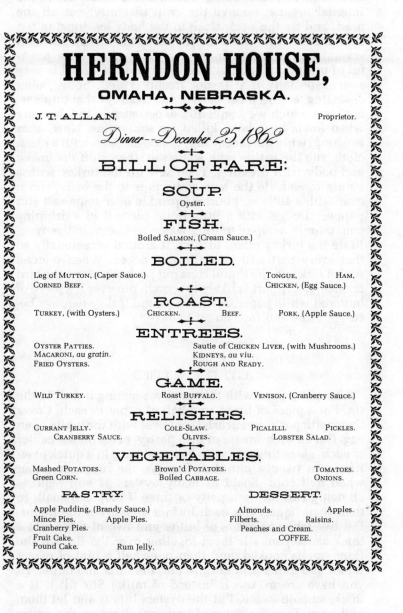

HERNDON HOUSE,
OMAHA, NEBRASKA.

J. T. ALLAN,   Proprietor.

Dinner--December 25, 1862

BILL OF FARE:

SOUP.
Oyster.

FISH.
Boiled SALMON, (Cream Sauce.)

BOILED.

Leg of MUTTON, (Caper Sauce.)	TONGUE, HAM,
CORNED BEEF.	CHICKEN, (Egg Sauce.)

ROAST.

TURKEY, (with Oysters.)   CHICKEN.   BEEF.   PORK, (Apple Sauce.)

ENTREES.

OYSTER PATTIES.	Sautie of CHICKEN LIVER, (with Mushrooms.)
MACARONI, *au gratin.*	KIDNEYS, *au viu.*
FRIED OYSTERS.	ROUGH AND READY.

GAME.

WILD TURKEY.   Roast BUFFALO.   VENISON, (Cranberry Sauce.)

RELISHES.

CURRANT JELLY.	COLE-SLAW.	PICALILLI.	PICKLES.
CRANBERRY SAUCE.	OLIVES.		LOBSTER SALAD.

VEGETABLES.

Mashed POTATOES.	Brown'd POTATOES.	TOMATOES.
Green CORN.	Boiled CABBAGE.	ONIONS.

PASTRY.	DESSERT.
Apple Pudding, (Brandy Sauce.)	Almonds. Apples.
Mince Pies. Apple Pies.	Filberts. Raisins.
Cranberry Pies.	Peaches and Cream.
Fruit Cake.	COFFEE.
Pound Cake. Rum Jelly.	

The Early Days   23 then draw it nicely, being careful not to break any of the internal organs; remove the crop carefully; cut off the head, and tie the neck close to the body by drawing the skin over it. Now rinse the inside of the turkey out with several waters, and in the next to the last, mix a teaspoonful of baking soda; oftentimes the inside of a fowl is very sour, especially if it is not freshly killed. Soda, being cleansing, acts as a corrective, and destroys that unpleasant taste which we frequently experience in the dressing when fowls have been killed for some time. Now, after washing, wipe the turkey dry, inside and out, with a clean cloth, rub the inside with some salt, then stuff the breast and body with dressing. Then sew up the turkey with a strong thread, tie the legs and wings to the body, rub it over with a little soft butter, sprinkle over some salt and pepper, dredge with a little flour; place it in a dripping pan, pour in a cup of boiling water, and set it in the oven. Baste the turkey often, turning it around occasionally so that every part will be uniformly baked. When pierced with a fork and the liquid runs out perfectly clear, the bird is done. If any part is likely to scorch, pin over it a piece of buttered white paper. A fifteen-pound turkey requires between three and four hours to bake.

OYSTER PATTIES

Line patty-pans with thin pastry, pressing it well to the tin. Put a piece of bread or a ball of paper in each. Cover them with paste and brush them over with the white of an egg. Cut an inch square of thin pastry, place on the center of each, glaze this also with egg, and bake in a quick oven fifteen to twenty minutes. Remove the bread or paper when half cold. Scald as many oysters as you require, allowing two for each patty or three if they are small, in their own liquor. Cut each in four and strain the liquor. Put two tablespoonfuls of butter and two of flour into a thick sauce-pan; stir them together over the fire till the flour smells cooked, and then pour half a pint of oyster liquor and half a pint of milk into the flour and butter. (If you have cream, use it instead of milk.) Stir till it is a thick, smooth sauce. Put the oysters into it and let them boil once. Beat the yolks of two eggs. Remove the oyster mixture for one minute from the fire, then stir the eggs into it till the sauce looks like thick custard. Fill the patties with this oyster fricassee, taking care to make it hot by standing it in boiling water before dinner on the day required, and to make the patty cases hot before you fill them.

ROASTED VENISON

Wash your venison clean, butter it well, and tie a piece of paper around it to prevent the juice from running out. It will take an hour and a half to roast a large haunch, or an hour for a small one.

PICCALILI

Mix together one peck of green tomatoes, peeled and chopped, and eight large onions, chopped fine, with one cup of salt well stirred in. Let it stand over night. In the morning drain off all the liquid; add two quarts of water and one of vinegar and boil all together twenty minutes. Drain through a seive or colander. Put it back into the kettle again; turn over it two quarts of vinegar, one pound of sugar, half a pound of white mustard seed, two tablespoonfuls of ground pepper, two of cinnamon, one of cloves, two of ginger, one of allspice, and half a teaspoonful of cayenne pepper. Boil fifteen minutes, or until tender, stirring often to prevent scorching, and seal in jars.

LOBSTER SALAD

Take a can of lobsters, skim off all the oil on the surface, and chop the meat up coarsely on a flat dish. Prepare the same way six heads of celery; mix a teaspoonful of mustard into a smooth paste with a little vinegar; add two fresh yolks of eggs, a tablespoonful of butter, creamed, a small teaspoonful of salt, the same of pepper, a quarter of a teaspoonful of cayenne pepper, a gill of vinegar, and the mashed yolks of two hard-boiled eggs. Mix a small portion of the dressings with the celery and meat, and turn the remainder over all. Garnish with the green tops of celery and a hard-boiled egg cut into thin rings.

POUND CAKE

Beat to a cream one pound of butter with one pound of sugar, and mix well with the beaten yolks of twelve eggs, one grated nutmeg, one wine-glass of wine, one wine-glass of rosewater. Then stir in one pound of sifted flour and the well-beaten whites of the eggs. Bake in a slow oven until a nice light brown. Can be kept for weeks in an earthen jar, closely covered, first dipping letter-paper in brandy and placing over the top of the cake before covering the jar.

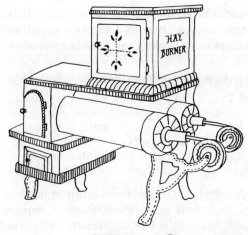

The Sod-House Period

ON JANUARY 1, 1863, exactly one week after that sumptuous holiday dinner at the Herndon House, Daniel Freeman ushered in a new era in Nebraska history by filing the first claim under the Homestead Act at the Brownville land office. Under the terms of the law, a person could acquire a quarter-section of public land by paying a ten-dollar filing fee and living on or cultivating his claim for five years. The prospect of free land and the coming of the railroad in 1866 and 1867 attracted tens of thousands of settlers, and in 1867 Nebraska was granted full-fledged statehood. For the next two decades the homesteaders would dominate the state's population and economy. Most of them came from agricultural areas to the east, but a large proportion immigrated from Europe, especially Germany, the British Isles, Scandinavia, and Bohemia. Almost universally, these newcomers started out with nothing but hope and hard work, building even their homes—sod houses or dugouts—literally from the land they lived on.

One of the first items that a homesteader installed in his soddy was a stove. A common early type used for both cooking and heating was designed to burn hay—hence its name, the hay burner—although corn cobs and buffalo and cow chips were also frequently used as fuel. Charley O'Kieffe, whose family homesteaded in the Sandhills in the 1880s, has described, "for the edification of housewives who may never have cooked with buffalo chips," the routine his mother went through in making baking powder biscuits:

> Stoke the stove, get out the flour sack, stoke the stove, wash your hands, mix the biscuit dough, stoke the stove, wash your hands, cut out the biscuits with the top of a baking-powder can, stoke the stove, wash your hands, put the pan of biscuits in the oven, keep on stoking the stove until the biscuits are done. Mother had to go through this tedious routine three times a day excepting when what she was cooking did not require the use of the oven.

The homeseekers brought their recipes and familiar methods of cooking with them, but their new circumstances required many adjustments. Like the settlers of the territorial period, they often lacked basic items and were forced to improvise. Mattie Oblinger, whose husband, Uriah, and brother Giles homesteaded in Fillmore County in 1872, wrote home to her sister in Indiana:

> You do not know how many things a person can do without until they try. Yesterday morning I thought I would have some cakes for dinner. I was going to make Jumbles but Giles had no rolling pin or cake cutter, so I made a plate of pancakes as we always turn it well. I had no eggs but I thought I would try it without. I tell you what I used—nearly a teacup of sugar, about half [a] teacup of cream filled up with water, a small lump of butter and a little soda, enough flour to make [the batter] quite stiff—and I never made any better pancakes in my life. Try it sometime. I make pancakes altogether without eggs. We used to think if we had no eggs we could not make pancakes, but I have got bravely over that.

Mattie also made biscuits without lard ("shortening is not the style here for biscuit"), and used water instead of milk in bread pudding. She reported that she regularly made salt-rising bread, a widespread practice among frontier housewives when they ran out of yeast.

SALT-RISING BREAD

Take about half a gallon of warm water; add to it salt, soda, and sugar, of each a lump about as large as an ordinary pea. A spoonful of corn meal improves it if convenient, though not necessary; stir in flour to the consistency of thick batter. A vessel holding about a gallon is most convenient, and it should be placed in a larger vessel and surrounded by warm water, and kept warm for four or five hours, when it will have become light, perhaps filling the vessel. If while it was kept in a warm place there should any water rise on it pour it off. Now that it is light get your flour into the kneading pan. Take about a pint of scalding water and scald part of the flour; then add enough cold water to cool the scalded flour; now add your rising and knead until smooth, but do not make it so stiff as for hop yeast bread. When the dough has become smooth mold and put it in your baking pans, and keep in a warm place to rise. When ready to bake it will require a hotter fire than for yeast bread. When baked wrap in a wet cloth and set away to cool.

At the end of summer, 1876, Mattie mentioned in one of her letters home that she and Uriah had been "plumming and grapering" on the Little Blue and planned to put up plum butter when they got their molasses made. Sorghum molasses was used extensively in place of sugar on the sod-house frontier. Charley O'Kieffe tells how it was made.

During two or three of our years on the Sheridan County farm, we raised a pretty fair patch of sorghum cane. When the proper time came in the fall, before the first killing frost, we stripped off the leaves and cut off the bunch of seeds at the top: the leaves would be used as fodder and the seeds as feed—mainly for the chickens. They relished these seeds, which also made them better layers. Then we cut down the naked stalks and loaded them on the wagon.

Old Man Hardy had set up a sorghum mill on his farm which was two miles east of us on the way to the Lone Butte, and there we hauled our cane stalks. (He had to call his outfit a sorghum mill because his son Rufus was a schoolteacher, and no common word like " 'lasses" would do in that family.) The mill was a simple affair consisting of a pair of steel rollers much like a clothes wringer except the rollers were larger and were set upright, not horizontally. As the canes were fed into them, they were rotated by a set of gears powered by an old horse hitched to a long sweep, which he pulled around and around in an endless circle.

The cane juice thus crushed out dropped down into a receptacle which was emptied at frequent intervals into the nearby cooking tank. This was made of galvanized sheet metal, and was six feet long by four feet wide and about ten inches deep. Below the tank was the firebox, which was stoked with every sort of heat-making material that could be found around the farm. The yellowish-green scum was skimmed off the top several times, and then the fully cooked molasses was drained off ready to be taken home in whatever type of container we could round up. As I recall, for his toil Old Man Hardy kept one gallon out of every four.

At home the molasses was stored away for winter use—and did it ever taste good! Maybe a bit strong for our tastes today, but it sure went well on breakfast pancakes, and we also mixed it with lard to make a spread for Mother's homemade bread. Altogether, it was a mighty big reward for planting an acre or so of cane and cultivating it along with the adjoining corn.

If we had only known about it, what wonderful taffy and other kinds of candy we might have made from our homegrown 'lasses. But what you don't know doesn't hurt you, so we never missed such treats.

Other sweeteners included imitation maple syrup made with corn cobs and—one of the most ingenious—boiled-down watermelon juice. A contributor to the volume *Sod House Memories* published by the Sod House Society gives this recipe.

CORN COB SYRUP

One dozen large, clean red cobs. Cover these with water; boil one to two hours. Drain off the water and strain it. There should be a pint of it. Add two pounds of brown sugar to this and boil to desired thickness.

Homesteaders acquired chickens, cows, and hogs as soon as possible, not only for their own food supply, but for produce to exchange for other goods. Mont Hawthorne, whose family took a claim on the Middle Loup River in the early 1870s, reminisced that during the panic of 1873, when money was scarce,

we tried to get by with using mighty little of it. When the hens was laying, Mama would send eggs to the store. She traded butter, too, but when she did we'd run short of it and of cream at home. Mama made awful good butter and storekeepers was always glad to get it because it never got rancid. She was terrible fussy about it and kept all the milk things clean and scalded. I had to help her and she'd make me churn hard at first and then slower after awhile so's it would come better and gather in bigger chunks. Mama always washed the edges of the churn down careful with cold water, and then she gathered every bit of the butter up with a wooden ladle made with holes in it so the buttermilk would drain off. She'd keep working the butter in a big wooden bowl with a wooden paddle, and she'd slap it and score it and wash it with cold water until every bit of buttermilk was out. Then she'd pack it into a square mold that was hinged on one corner and that had been scalded good and dipped in cold water so the butter wouldn't stick to it. And it would come out in the nicest, hardest bricks you ever seen. Them rolls weighed two pound and she'd wrap them in muslin and tie them with a string, and mostly send them along with Father to trade for our other provisions. But whenever Mama could, she'd hold one out and put it down for winter in a crock that was full of brine made of salt strong enough to float an egg.

In the summer,

after the weather turned hot, Mama said she knowed, no matter
how careful she packed it, the butter would get rancid while it
was being hauled over sixty mile to Grand Island. Father said
he'd seen butter throwed out along the road because the
storekeepers wouldn't take it. And Mama said she wasn't making butter for the coyotes and wolves to clean up, so she had him
bring out a big crateful of them heavy crocks that holds six
gallon apiece, and she'd make butter, and work it until every
drop of buttermilk was out. She'd salt it good and pack it down
in one of them crocks. By fall she had a whole row of them
buried in a deep trench down by the spring, with lids fastened
down tight to shut out the air, and several inches of dirt piled on
top to help keep them cool. We'd bury them crocks just as fast as
we filled them and that way the butter never had a chance to get
rancid. When cold weather came, Father took them crocks of
butter in to Grand Island and Mama went along with her list of
what we needed for food and clothing for the winter, and she
outfitted and provisioned us because that butter was blamed
good and it was sent right out to Leadville and Denver and sold
as fresh butter and it brung ten cents a pound, which was considerable above the regular market. But, of course, us children
didn't have no way of knowing that our butter-making would
pay off so good when we was working with the milk during
them hot summer days on our homestead out there at Arcadia.

Mont's enterprising mother found another use for the extra
milk from the family's herd:

Mama'd read a book about cheese-making. Then the fellow
from Grand Island, who helped make them big vats to hold the
milk, taught her what he knowed. He let a calf suck until it
couldn't hold no more milk. Then he killed it, took out its
stomach, washed it good, and hung it in the sunshine to sour.
The stuff inside the calf's stomach turned out to be rennit, that
we had to put in the fresh milk to make it curdle. I never knowed
they made cheese like that. Blamed if it didn't make my stomach
curdle, just watching him.

Eggs were kept in a number of different ways—by coating
with paraffin, storing in brine, packing in barrels of sawdust
stored in a cool place, or preserving in borax. The point of all
these methods was to provide an air-tight seal.

TO KEEP EGGS

Make a solution of borax water—a heaping teaspoonful of pulverized borax to a pint of boiling water—let stand until the solution becomes warm, but do not allow it to so cool that the borax will crystallize; dip the eggs quickly then. Keep in a cool place; the borax will crystallize around the egg, therefore keep out the air and preserve the egg.

Since pork in its many forms—ham, bacon, salted side pork (or sowbelly, as it was commonly known), sausage, and head cheese—was the principal meat as well as the source of lard for shortening and soap, butchering day was a red-letter occasion. "Among the many workaday chores most young men had to learn was the messy but necessary job of butchering," writes Charley O'Kieffe. "This was how you got your diploma:"

First, you honed the family butcher knife to razor-edge sharpness; next, the victim was brought to the scene of operations and the scalding barrel filled. Then came the big moment: you had to plunge the knife into the porker's throat at just the right spot and at just the right angle so that the point would enter his heart. When this was done properly, the hog would stagger about for a minute and then drop dead. Now you grasped him by his hind feet and soused him repeatedly into scalding water, the scalding barrel being set at an angle so the carcass could be pulled out and shoved back with the greatest possible ease. When the hair had been sufficiently loosened up, you then scraped him entirely free of it. Usually this was done with a very sharp corn knife—an implement which, because of its length and fine steel, could be used for a variety of other things than cutting corn fodder.

After he got his clean shave, the hog was prepared for the gallows and last rites. A slit was made in each hind leg just a little above the hoof, and the strong sinew found there was spread away from the leg to make an opening into which the end of the gambrel was inserted. Made of strong wood usually salvaged from a broken or worn-out singletree, the gambrel was long enough to spread the hind legs wide and strong enough to hold the heaviest hog. It was hooked over the end of an elevated pole or wagon tongue, thus raising the carcass off the ground for evisceration. (Gutting was our word for it.)

Almost anyone could carry out the final phases of butchering—cutting up the carcass and putting away the hams, shoulders, side meat, etc. Some of the meat would be smoked if facilities were available, or salted down and stored, or given to neighbors on a lend-lease basis. Because cash money was scarce, I do not recall of any sales being made, although trading and outright gifts were very common. If a butchered animal was to be sold, it had to be hauled to town and there disposed of for some cash and the rest in trade.

A smokehouse could be improvised from an inverted barrel with holes bored in the sides for the insertion of sticks on which the ham was hung. The barrel was placed over a smoky fire in a small trench; and after smoking, the hams were wrapped in gunny sacks coated with a flour paste to form an airtight covering. The *Nebraska Farmer* carried these instructions for smoking bacon.

TO SMOKE BACON

Take a tin pan or kettle of corn cobs and set them on the fire so as to make them smoke; then turn bottom side up over the smoking cobs the barrel, or whatever you wish to pickle or salt your bacon in, so as to thoroughly smoke the inside of it. Burn at least two pans of cobs under it, so as to smoke it well. Then pack the hams, shoulders, or other meat that you wish to make bacon of, in the cask, and after preparing your pickle heat it nearly boiling hot, and pour it on the meat and let the meat stay until it is pickled, when it is made into bacon, ready for use and well smoked. The bacon can remain in the pickle until used, and you can watch the pickle in the summer, and should it ferment, scald it over.

Scrapple made with fresh organ meats, sausage or pork cake, and souse, or pickled pigs' feet, were butchering-time dishes.

SCRAPPLE

Take the head, heart, and any lean scraps of pork, and boil until the flesh slips easily from the bones. Remove the fat, gristle, and bones, then chop fine. Set the liquor in which the meat was boiled aside until cold, take the cake of fat from the surface, and return to the fire. When it boils, put in the chopped meat and season well with salt and pepper. Thicken with cornmeal as you would in making ordinary cornmeal mush. Cook an hour, stirring constantly at first, afterwards putting back on the stove to boil gently. When done, pour into pans and mold. In cold weather this can be kept several weeks. Cut into slices and fry brown as you do mush.

PORK FRUIT CAKE

One pound of pork, one cup molasses, two cups sugar, one pint boiling water, two eggs, one tablespoon each of cinnamon, cloves, and allspice, two teaspoons cream of tartar, one teaspoon of soda, one pound of raisins, chopped, flour to make it the consistency of any stirred cake. Chop the pork fine and pour on the boiling water; let stand until no longer hot. Bake very slowly. The longer the cake is kept, the better it becomes.

PICKLED PIGS' FEET (SOUSE)

Scrape and clean the pigs' feet thoroughly. Put in kettle and boil for four or five hours until soft. Add salt to taste during boiling. Take out and pack in a crock or stone jar. Boil vinegar and spice it well; pour over pigs' feet until covered. Allow them to stand for several days before serving.

To serve, split them, make a batter of two eggs, a cup of milk, salt, a teaspoonful of butter, with flour enough to make a thick batter. Dip each piece in this and fry in hot lard, or dip them in beaten egg and flour and fry. Good eaten cold or warm.

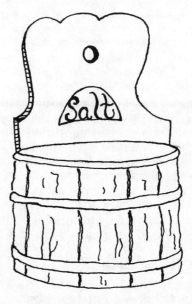

Fried chicken—"parson food," it was called, because it was inevitably served when the preacher came to dinner —remained company fare until well after the turn of the century. Getting the bird from the chicken coop to the dinner table was no mean art. Again Charley O'Kieffe elaborates:

While the young man in the family was taking his lessons in butchering and other branches of animal husbandry, his sister or girl friend was getting used to, and learning the knack of, chopping off the head of some ancient rooster or an old biddy hen who had signed her own death warrant by falling down on egg-laying, her real mission in life. After decapitation with a sharp axe on the chopping block out by the wood pile, the victim was allowed to flop around for a minute or two, so as to complete the bleeding process. Then the fowl would be doused in scalding water to loosen its feathers, after which the larger, coarser ones would be plucked. Next the young lady would find herself a fairly big piece of paper, set it afire on top of the stove, and rotate the plucked fowl in the flames at just the proper height to singe off the remaining feathers, especially the tiny pinfeathers that could not be removed by hand plucking.

After all the entrails were removed through a slit [around] the fowl's back door, the empty hull was washed out with cold water. Great care had to be taken to see that the gizzard was not cut or broken open and its contents scattered about in the chicken's body. The gizzard contains an assortment of items —bits of glass, grains of sand, small pieces of metal—which are useful in the living fowl's digestive process, but very destructive to the flavor of the cooked fowl. After the gizzard has been removed and the chicken split open and thoroughly cleaned, it (the gizzard) can safely be reunited with the rest of the fowl to be cooked in the manner best adapted to that particular bird and to the family's taste.

FRIED CHICKEN

Wash and cut up the chicken, wipe it dry, season with salt and pepper, dredge it with flour, or dip each piece in beaten egg and then in cracker crumbs. Have the lard hot in the frying pan and lay in the chicken. When brown on both sides, take up, drain, and set aside in a covered dish. Stir into the gravy left a large tablespoonful of flour, make it smooth, add a cup of cream or milk, season with salt and pepper, boil up and pour over the chicken.

If the chicken is old, put into a stew pan with a little water and simmer gently till tender. Season with salt and pepper, dip in flour or cracker crumbs and egg, and fry as above. Use the broth the chicken was cooked in to make the gravy instead of cream or milk, or use an equal quantity of both.

In season, weeds such as pigweed, lambsquarters, and purslane added variety to the homesteaders' diet, Charley tells us ("In the O'Kieffe home, our slogan was: 'If you can't beat'em, eat'em' ").

Mother had a way of slipping a small hunk of salt pork in the pot with the cooking weeds and, brother, that made the difference. . . . Since those days of long ago I have eaten collards in the Deep South and mustard greens in Kentucky, to say nothing of lobsters in Maine, oysters in the many bars in New Orleans, and broiled Spanish mackerel in Gulfport, Mississippi, but none of their dishes tasted any better than did the weeds of Northwestern Nebraska back in the 1880's. Why? Because I was hungry then as I have never been hungry since.

In his account of the "edible Flora" of his area, Charley also includes

red and blue plums, wild grapes, chokecherries, and currants both yellow and blue. These could be found in almost every section along or near the Niobrara River. But the two most remarkable fruits, the likes of which I have never found anywhere else, were the sand cherry and the buffalo berry.

In its body composition the sand cherry is fibrous, made up of the same vegetable growth as a cherry tree, but instead of growing upward it sprawls out more like a vine. As it nearly always lives in the vicinity of an actual or potential blowout, there are times when this unusual plant is entirely covered with sand. Nevertheless, it keeps right on growing, and many a time have I pulled on one sand cherry only to pull the rest of the plant out of the loose sand with a dozen or two big luscious berries attached to the branch on which I thought there was but one. The fruit itself is about the same size as a Bing cherry, and is just as beautiful and inviting to look at, but it is puckery to the taste and except when dead-ripe has to be treated before it is edible.

We gathered them by the washtub-full at picking time, and took them home where they were pitted . . . and then dried in the bright sun until they looked quite like small scraps of chamois skin that had become soiled by handling. While I do not recall having eaten any chamois skin, I think it must taste something like these dried bits of sand cherry. But times Mother had gotten a little extra trade value out of her butter and eggs at the Rushville store, she would bring home a small lot of dried apples, and when five or six of these were added to a gallon of the dried sand cherries we children ate them gladly to get the apples.

The buffalo berry almost defies description both as to its growing habits and the fruit it produces. The trees—or rather large bushes—were none too plentiful and when the berries were ready for picking there was likely to be plenty of competition. Usually found along the Niobrara River, these shrubs had such an odd color and shape that they could be easily spotted by anyone who knew what to look for. The gray, almost white, leaves were long and narrow, much like the leaves of the better grade of China tea. The bushes themselves were thorned, like some plum trees, but the fruit itself was small, brilliant red, and very acid. It clung to the mother bush as long as possible, and the best time to gather these berries was right after the first frost. You harvested them by spreading a sheet around under the bush and beating the branches until the fruit fell off into it. Generally the ingathering was none too plentiful, but what we got was well worth the labor.

Those of us who could dig up enough sugar made jelly out of the bulk of our berries, saving a few for sauce. Made without any modern pectin ingredients, buffalo-berry jelly was very transparent and could almost pass the old test for clarity—being able to read a newspaper through a glass of it. We had no newspaper to make the test with, but this didn't stop us from enjoying and admiring the jelly. There may be a domesticated buffalo berry now, but I have never found one in any seed catalog that bore any resemblance to the wild buffalo berry.

I could not write about our Flora without saying some nice words about the "sarvisberry." Where the mixed-up races of mankind who made up the early settlers of the West got this word I have no idea, but I do know where and when we found the berries, and how delicious they were. In general, they were quite like the blueberry. Starting out as green, they turned red and finally a rich almost transparent blue. At the outer end of each berry were three little leaves. Their habitat was along the lower slope of the hills just south of the Niobrara and before you reached the actual sandhills—there they did not seem to do so well. The shrub grew to varying heights, but was never so tall that it was any problem to pick the fruit. In fact, the serviceberry was about the easiest of all berries to find if you knew where it grew, and the most suitable for eating after you had picked it —rich and mellow, sweet but not sickeningly so, meaty and not too juicy, and just plain perfect whether fresh with cream, stewed into sauce, or baked in pie.

CURRANT JELLY

Strip the currants off the stem, and bruise them thoroughly; put on the fire to heat, and when at boiling point strain them. To a pint of juice allow a pound of loaf sugar. When the mixture begins to boil again, let it boil just fifteen minutes.

Charley's observation—"Ever since the Divine Creator set the Universe spinning, man has depended on the good earth for his food, his raiment, and his equipment; and on our . . . farm we certainly did find it the only source of things to keep soul and body together with"—could have applied to virtually all Nebraska homesteaders. But though their resources were limited to what they raised, gathered, traded for, or received in those rare, treasured packages from the folks back home, sod-house cooks, like their modern counterparts, avidly collected and exchanged recipes, even for dishes they would likely not prepare (how many could afford oranges, or coconut, or pistachio nuts, or had the wherewithal to whip up a puff paste?). All of the following are taken from authentic Nebraska sources of the sod-house era; most appeared in the *Nebraska Farmer* or local newspapers, a few are from the cookbooks of homestead wives.

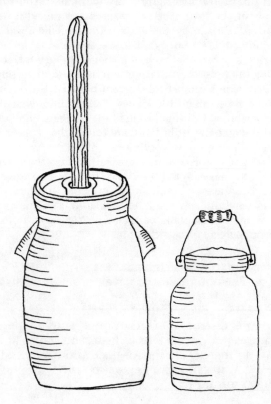

CENTENNIAL BISCUIT (MUSH ROLLS)

Make good corn mush, just as if you were going to eat it with milk; when it is lukewarm take a quart of it, work in flour enough to make a stiff dough, make it into biscuits, put in your bake pan, and set it in a warm place over night. Bake in a very hot oven, and you have the best and sweetest biscuit you ever ate. Eat while hot for breakfast.

GRAHAM BREAD

Prepare a sponge as for white bread; put into your baking pan the next morning a proportionate quantity of flour, two-thirds graham and one-third white, to every quart of which you will allow a large handful of Indian meal and a teaspoonful of salt. Make a hole in the center of this and pour in your sponge, with two tablespoonfuls of molasses for each medium-sized loaf. The dough must be very soft. It will take a longer time to rise than white bread; when light, knead again, make into loaves, and set in a warm place for a second raising. Bake steadily in a moderate oven for a much longer time than you would allow for white bread. Rapid baking will spoil it. In this, as in most housekeeping duties, you must acquire judgment by experience. The most essential point in the making of the dough is to keep it very soft.

RYE BREAD

Take one quart of warm water, one teacupful of yeast, and thicken with rye flour. Put in a warm place to rise overnight. In the morning scald—well cook—one pint of Indian meal. When cool, add to the sponge, with salt, a little molasses, a pint of warm water, and rye flour to knead very soft. Let rise, then put into pans. Again let rise, then bake. The dough should never be molded stiff for rye bread, and, if preferred, the flour may be wholly worked in with an iron spoon instead of the hands.

BUTTERMILK BREAD

Bring two quarts of buttermilk to a boil and pour over two quarts of flour, stirring rapidly or it will be lumpy.

The Sod-House Period   41

Then add cold water until it is thin enough (it should be as thin as it can be stirred). If it is not cool enough for the yeast by this time, set the pail which it is in in the water pail, stirring it all the while, which soon cools it. Then stir in the yeast, which is already soaked, and empty it all in the bread pan, where the flour is already warm, with a hole in the middle. Cover it tight where it will keep warm all night. The quicker the mixing is done, the better the bread will be. In the morning shape and bake the loaves as usual.

PARKER HOUSE ROLLS

At night take two quarts of flour, rub in three tablespoons of lard, make a hole in the middle and put in one pint of cold boiled milk, half a cup of yeast, three tablespoons sugar, one egg, and a teaspoon of salt. Let it stand until morning without mixing, then mix and let it stand until noon. Then roll out, cut into rolls, let them get very light, and bake in a quick oven.

APPLE BREAD

Weigh out one pound of fresh, juicy apples; peel, core, and stew them into a pulp, being careful to use a porcelain kettle or stone jar placed in a kettle of boiling water. Mix the pulp with two pounds of the best flour; put in the same quantity of yeast you would use for common bread, and as much water as will make it a fine, smooth dough. Put it into a pan and place it in a warm place to rise, and let it remain for twelve hours at least. Form it into rather long-shaped loaves, and bake in a quick oven.

SODA BISCUITS

Take four large cups of sifted flour, in which one large teaspoon soda and two teaspoons cream of tartar have been well mixed, with one teaspoon salt; add one-half cup butter and mix thoroughly; to this add a pint of sweet milk, a little at a time, and mix with as little kneading as possible. Bake in a quick oven eight to ten minutes.

MUFFINS

Two eggs, well beaten with a cupful of sugar, and a lump of butter the size of an egg; to this add one pint of milk, with a teaspoon of soda, one quart of flour, and two teaspoons of cream of tartar. Bake in muffin rings or in gem pans in a quick oven.

GRAHAM MUFFINS

Two cups of graham flour, one cup white flour, two eggs, two tablespoons of baking powder, milk to make a thin batter. Bake in a quick oven.

EGG PANCAKE

Beat six eggs light, add some salt and one pint of flour, and stir in gradually enough milk to make a thin, smooth batter. Make hot a griddle or skillet, butter the bottom, and put in enough batter to run over it as thin as a dollar piece. When brown turn it. When done take it out on a dish; put a little butter, sugar, and cinnamon over it. Fry another and treat likewise, and so on until a plate is piled. Send hot to the table for dessert, or breakfast, or tea.

BUCKWHEAT CAKES

Mix one gill of wheat flour with one quart of buckwheat flour, and one large tablespoonful of salt, then add gradually a scant quart of warm water mixed with one gill of yeast. Let it rise all night, and in the morning add a quarter of a teaspoonful of carbonate of soda, and bake immediately on a smooth, well-greased iron griddle, taking care to scrape it well after each baking, and using as little grease as possible. The cakes should not be larger than a small saucer, and should be served at once.

DROP CAKES FOR SUPPER

Rub together four tablespoonfuls of sugar and one of butter, and add two well-beaten eggs, a little salt and one-half pint of milk. Stir in flour sufficient to make a batter nearly as stiff as for cake. Sift one tablespoonful of sea foam or baking powder through the flour before making the batter. Bake as muffins on a hot griddle. Butter lightly and eat hot. Children are very fond of them, and eaten in moderation they are quite harmless, even at night.

DOUGHNUTS

Three eggs, two cupfuls of sugar, one and one-half cupfuls of milk, butter the size of a small egg, two teaspoonfuls cream of tartar rubbed into a quart of flour, one teaspoonful soda dissolved in milk, a little salt, and one half nutmeg. Use flour enough to roll out soft; cut in fancy shapes, and drop into boiling lard. A slice of raw potato put in the fat will prevent it from burning.

CRACKERS

To make good and healthful crackers, take, for five cups of good flour, one cup of melted butter; rub it well into the flour; then put one teaspoonful of soda in a bowl and pour a little warm water on it and dissolve; have ready two teaspoonfuls of cream of tartar, and put a cupful of cold water into the bowl that has the soda in it. When ready to turn into the flour, add the cream of tartar, and pour in while it is effervescing. Mix your dough and roll out half as thick as a cracker ought to be, and cut in squares or small rounds. Bake in a well-heated oven.

CRUSHED WHEAT

Sort out two or three teacupfuls of wheat, then grind it on a hand mill or a coffee mill. Stir the meal into boiling water in an iron pot or skillet and cook until done. If the meal is ground coarse, it requires longer cooking than when ground fine. Add a little salt. Serve hot and eat with sweetened milk on.

CORN SOUP

One pint of corn, one pint boiling water, one pint milk, one slice of onion, two tablespoons butter, two table-

44   *Nebraska Pioneer Cookbook*

spoons flour, one teaspoon salt, few grains pepper. Chop the corn, add the water, and simmer twenty minutes; run through a sieve. Scald the milk with the onion, remove onion, and add the milk to the corn. Bind with butter and flour cooked together. Add salt and pepper.

TOMATO SOUP

Have a gallon of nice stock from fresh beef, skim off the top, add two quart cans of tomatoes, put through a fine sieve, make a paste of half a teaspoonful of flour with butter enough to mix, and stir into the soup as it boils. To prevent its being lumpy, take out a little of the soup and mix first with it. Boil twenty minutes. Season with pepper and salt.

A CHEAP VEGETABLE SOUP

The following is the recipe given by the celebrated Francatelli for a cheap vegetable soup: Put six quarts of water to boil in a large pot with a quarter of a pound of suet or two ounces of drippings (cost about two cents), season it with a level tablespoonful of salt, half a teaspoonful of pepper, and a few sprigs of parsley and dried herbs (cost of seasoning one cent). While it is boiling prepare about ten cents' worth of cabbage, turnips, beans, or any cheap vegetables in season; throw them into the boiling soup, and, when they have boiled up thoroughly, set the pot at the side of the fire, where it will simmer for about two hours. Then take up some of the vegetables without breaking, and use them with any gravy you may have on hand or with a quarter of a pound of bacon (cost four cents), sliced and fried, for the bulk of the meal. The soup, after being seasoned to taste, can be eaten with bread, at the beginning of the meal, the whole of which can be provided for about twenty cents.

CHICKEN SOUP

One chicken, four quarts of water, one tablespoon of rice, one onion, one potato, one turnip, one-half cup of tomatoes, two stalks of celery, pepper and salt to taste. Put on the chicken in cold water, and boil to shreds. Strain the broth, return to the kettle and add rice, and in about half an hour add potato, onion, and turnip chopped fine. About twenty minutes before serving add the celery cut into small pieces, the tomato, and pepper and salt. Boil well, and serve very hot, and you will have a delicious soup.

WHITE SOUP

Boil a knuckle of veal and four calves' feet in five quarts of water, with three onions sliced, a bunch of sweet herbs, four blades of white celery, cut small, a tablespoonful of whole pepper, and a tablespoonful of salt, adding five or six large blades of mace. Let it boil very slowly, till the meat is in rags and has dropped from the bone, and till the gristle has quite dissolved. Skim it well while boiling. When done, strain it through a sieve into a tureen or a deep whiteware pan. Next day take off all the fat and put the jelly (for such it ought to be) into a clean soup pot, with two ounces of tapioca, and set it over the fire. When the pearl tapioca is dissolved, stir in, gradually, a pint of thick cream, while the soup is quite hot; but do not let it come to a boil after the cream is in lest it should curdle. Cut up one or two rolls in the bottom of the tureen, pour in the soup, and send it to the table.

GAME SOUP (CLEAR)

Take the remnants of any kind of game not high, put them in a saucepan with an onion and carrot, two or three cloves, a small piece of mace, a bay leaf, some parsley, and salt and pepper to taste. Cover the whole with veal or poultry stock, and set the saucepan to boil gently for a couple of hours. Strain off the soup and set it to boil again, then throw in an ounce of raw beef or liver coarsely chopped. Let it give one boil, and strain the soup through a napkin. A very small quantity of sherry may be put in before serving.

BROWN SOUP

Brown one tablespoonful of flour; put it in a bowl with a small lump of butter; stir together to a smooth paste and add a half pint of boiling water with a slice of toasted bread cut in small pieces, and salt to taste. This is palatable and nutritious, and when animal food is forbidden, takes the place of meat soups.

CHICKEN PIE

An old chicken will do for this purpose—in fact, it is preferable to a very young one. Singe and draw the fowl, cutting it up in joints. Cover with cold water, and let it simmer, closely covered, for an hour or more, according to its age. Then add three medium-sized onions sliced, some sprigs of parsley, and salt and pepper, and continue the cooking until the meat is tender and the onions done. Dish the bulky pieces, such as the back, under part of the breast, and first joints. Make a batter with one egg, a cup of milk, and a teaspoonful of sea foam or baking powder sifted through enough flour to make it of cup cake consistency. Drop this into the boiling broth in small spoonfuls. While the dumplings are cooking, which will take about eight minutes, heat to boiling half a pint of milk; pour this into the gravy after the rest of the meat and the dumplings have been removed, and stir in a lump of butter and a large tablespoonful of flour wet with a little cold milk; boil for a minute and pour over the chicken. The dumplings should be served on a separate dish. Bake a piece of rich piecrust the size of a dinner plate, break into as many pieces as there are people to be served, and place as a border around the dish containing the meat. This is chicken pie par excellence, and if your family is large you need not be afraid to prepare two chickens. If any is left, heat for breakfast; add a little soup stock, or thickened hot milk, if more gravy is necessary; and pour the whole over some slices of buttered toast. If the fowl is old and fat it would be advisable to remove as much as possible of the fat and skin before cooking.

CHICKEN PANADA

Skin the chicken and cut it up in joints. Take all the meat off the bones and cut up into small pieces; put it in a jar with a little salt, tie it down, and set it in a saucepan of boiling water. It should boil from four to six hours; then pass it through a sieve with a little of the broth. It could be made in a hurry in two hours, but it is better when longer time is allowed. Do not put the wings in the panada.

SMOKED GEESE BREASTS

Our German friends will relish this recipe and also the directions for making sour goose, which follow it. Cut out the breasts of young, fat, and well-cleaned geese, rub them well with salt and a little saltpeter, place in a jar or other vessel, with a weight upon them. Let them remain thus for ten days, after which put them in smoke for two weeks.

To utilize the remainder of the goose after cutting out the breast for smoking, it is prepared as follows: Cut up the flesh into suitable pieces, then take of vinegar and water, of equal quantities, enough to cover the meat; add a handful of small onions and salt, pepper, cloves, etc.; boil together until the meat is done. This, if put in a cool place, will keep well, and makes an excellent dish when warmed up or eaten cold.

ROAST PARTRIDGES

Pick, draw, singe, and truss the birds, placing a slice of bacon over the breast of each. Roast at a moderate fire, removing the bacon for a few minutes before the birds are done. Serve with plain gravy and bread sauce in boats.

ROAST WILD DUCKS

Pluck, draw, singe, and truss the birds. Wrap them in bacon and roast at a brisk fire for ten to fifteen minutes; serve with bigrade sauce: Pare off as thin as possible the yellow rind of two oranges, cut it into very thin shreds, and boil them in water for five minutes. Melt a piece of butter in a saucepan; add to it a tablespoonful of flour and stir until it begins to color; add a gill of stock, pepper and salt to taste, the juice of the oranges, and a good pinch of sugar; then put in the boiled rinds, stir the sauce until it boils, and serve.

The Sod-House Period   49

BEEFSTEAK

Always broil it. Have it cut half an inch or more in thickness. If not tender, pound it; see that there are plenty of hot coals, and broil quickly upon a gridiron, turning often. My rule is to broil twelve minutes, turning five or six times. Use beef tongs to turn with, as a fork will let out the juices. Take up on a platter, putting a little salt and butter on each side of the steak. Serve immediately.

STUFFED BEEF

Take the thin, flabby pieces on the fore quarter. Make a stuffing the same as for turkey, spread it on and roll tightly. Boil in salted water until nearly tender, and the water nearly boiled away; then add a little butter and stew down. To be sliced and eaten cold without unrolling. This can be roasted instead of boiled, if preferred.

BEEFSTEAK A LA PARISIENNE

Take a piece of rump steak about three-quarters of an inch thick; trim it neatly, and beat with the cuttle bat; sprinkle it with pepper, dip it in oil, and broil it over a clear fire. Turn it after it has been on the fire a minute or two, and keep turning it until done; eight or ten minutes will do it. Sprinkle with salt, and serve with a small quantity of finely minced parsley and a piece of butter mixed together and placed over or under the steak. Garnish with fried potatoes.

MEAT PIE

Have the meat perfectly tender and remove all the bones. Cut it into small pieces, but do not hash it. Unless some of the meat is fat, add butter the size of half an egg. Add a little more water than will cover it. Season with pepper and salt, and slice in one or two onions according to quantity. Heat, then stir a heaping teaspoonful of flour into a little water, as for starch, and thicken the water. If you have macaroni, break up a few sticks and add; otherwise slice in two or three potatoes. Pour into a deep baking dish; make a crust as for rich biscuit and lay over the top. Cut a place in the center for steam to escape, and bake half or three-quarters of an hour in a moderate oven.

HASH

Chop a couple of small onions and put with a little water into a skillet or small kettle; cook till tender and nearly dry; add a cupful of chopped meat, and a little more than a cupful of mashed or chopped cold potatoes; Put in a good piece of butter, and salt and pepper to taste. Stir all together, heat hot, and serve at once.

BOILED HAM

Boil a small corned—not smoked—ham. When tender, cut out the bone from one end, peel off the skin, cover the outside with beaten egg, and dust thickly with fine cracker crumbs. Put into the oven and leave there until the grease from the ham penetrates the crackers and the entire top is brown and crisp. This way of preparing ham looks much more inviting than the common way of removing the skin alone without glazing with egg and cracker.

FRIED LIVER

Cut liver into small strips, put on a platter, pour over boiling water and immediately pour it off. Place a frying pan on the stove with some beef drippings in it, dredge the liver with cracker dust, season with pepper and salt, and put into the pan. Cover and fry slowly until the pieces are well browned. A little chopped onion cooked with the liver is very nice for those who like the flavor.

SHEEP'S PLUCK

Cut the liver and lights [lungs] in thin slices and put them in a pie dish or jar, with layers of sliced potato and onion, chopped sage and herbs, pepper, and salt. A few slices of bacon may be added. Cover with a thin piece of suet or with greased paper and bake one and a half hours. Where there is no oven, this may be stewed.

SCALLOPED MUTTON

Cut cold roast mutton into bits, removing all skin and gristle. If you have no gravy, make it by stewing the scraps and bones in a little water, then season with pepper, salt, and tomato catsup, and strain it over the meat. Boil some potatoes and mash them while hot until they are free from lumps, then beat with a fork until white and light; add a lump of butter, some milk, and lastly a beaten egg. Mix well, then place the meat in a pudding dish, spread the mashed potato, which should be quite soft, smoothly on top, brush it evenly with a beaten egg, and bake it in a quick oven until it is a beautiful golden brown. This makes an excellent breakfast dish, and can be prepared ready for baking the night before. Especial care should be taken to have plenty of gravy, as it is absorbed in cooking, and the dish will not be so palatable if too dry. Cold roast beef may be prepared in the same manner. In making the gravy, be careful to remove the fat before pouring it over the meat.

SCALLOPED OYSTERS

Scald one quart of oysters in their liquor, drain them, remove the beards, and place them in a scalloped shell that has been well buttered and bread crumbed. Melt in a saucepan one large tablespoonful of butter, stir in one teaspoonful of flour, cook a little, add one gill of broth and enough of the oyster liquor as to make the sauce of the consistency of cream, boil gently eight minutes, and add half a teaspoonful of chopped parsley, pour it over the oysters, sprinkle bread crumbs over them, lay one or two bits of butter on top, and bake ten or twelve minutes.

FISH CROQUETTES

Take some remnants of boiled fish, pick out the flesh carefully, and mince it not too finely. Melt a piece of butter in a saucepan; add a little flour and some hot milk. Stir on the fire until the mixture thickens, add pepper and salt, a little grated nutmeg and some chopped parsley, lastly the fish; and as soon as the mixture is quite hot turn it out on a dish to get cold. Shape it into the shape of corks, roll them in a beaten-up egg and then in baked bread crumbs; repeat the process in an hour's time, fry them in hot lard, and serve with fried parsley.

CODFISH CREAM

Pick in shreds one pound of boneless [salted] codfish and soak it over night in cold water. Do not let it freshen too much. In the morning put in a saucepan nearly a pint of milk, and when it boils stir in an even tablespoonful of corn starch dissolved in cold milk. Cook until the raw taste is gone, and then break in three eggs; let them stand a moment and then stir as for scrambled eggs. Add the picked fish, let it come to a boil, and if it gets too thick add half a cup of cream or rich milk. This makes a very tempting breakfast for those who are fond of the various preparations of salt cod. Chopped parsley and pepper may be added to taste.

GRATED HAM SANDWICHES

Grate finely as much well-cooked ham as you are likely to require; flavor it with a very little cayenne and some nutmeg. Roll out some good puff paste very thin, cut it into two perfectly even portions, prick in one or two places to prevent its rising too high, and bake in a quick oven till of a golden brown. Then take out and let it stand till cool, when spread a little fresh butter lightly over the whole. This should not be done till the paste is perfectly cool. Now spread the grated ham over it, and with a very sharp knife cut into small-sized sandwiches. This is a charming supper dish.

HAM AND EGG PUDDING

Six eggs beaten very light, a light pint of flour, a pint of milk, a small piece of butter, salt and pepper to the taste. Sprinkle some slices of boiled ham (both fat and lean) with pepper, and lay them across a deep dish that has been greased; then pour the pudding batter over it and bake quickly.

BAKED OMELETTE

Heat a quart of milk, reserving enough cold to wet smooth two tablespoonfuls of flour and two teaspoonfuls of salt. Beat eight eggs very light, add the flour, then the hot milk, stirring fast all the time. Then turn all into a buttered dish and bake twenty minutes to half an hour in a hot oven, or till it is handsomely browned.

The Sod-House Period   53

EGG SANDWICHES

Boil fresh eggs five minutes; put them in cold water, and when quite cold peel them; then, after taking a little white off each end of the eggs, cut the remainder in four slices. Lay them between bread and butter.

STUFFED EGGS

Six hard-boiled eggs cut in two, take out the yolks and mash fine; then add two teaspoonfuls of butter, one of cream, two or three drops of onion juice, salt and pepper to taste. Mix all thoroughly and fill the eggs with this mixture; put them together. Then there will be a little of the filling left, to which add one well-beaten egg. Cover the eggs with this mixture, and then roll in cracker crumbs. Fry a light brown in boiling fat.

CURRIED EGGS

Cut a couple of onions in slices and fry them to a light golden color in plenty of butter, add one tablespoonful of curry powder and a sprinkling of flour, moisten with a cupful of stock, and simmer gently for ten minutes. Then add six hard-boiled eggs cut in slices, simmer for a few minutes longer, and serve.

TARTELETTE AU PARMESAN

Take the yolks of two very fresh eggs, three dessert spoonfuls of cream, a little cayenne pepper, two dessert spoonfuls of fine grated Parmesan cheese, a little salt; beat these ingredients into a smooth paste. Make some tartlets of puff paste, fill them with the above mixture, and bake in the oven till of a light gold color.

DELICIOUS CHEESE

This is almost like "store cheese." Scald two gallons of sour milk, then strain it. Add one and one-half teaspoonfuls soda and one-half cup butter to curd. Let stand two hours. Place in double boiler and add two teaspoonfuls salt. Stir and add one cup very sour cream and cook half an hour or until thick. Then mold in bowl or jar. The acid in old butter and sour cream will add tang to the cheese. Yellow coloring may be added.

A VERY SIMPLE DISH OF MACARONI

Stew the requisite quantity of macaroni in some new milk, with salt to taste, till perfectly tender. Drain it carefully and place in a stewpan with a good lump of butter, stir round gently over the fire, and just before serving stir a couple of well-beaten eggs into the macaroni. Do not let it remain long enough over the fire to let it curdle, but serve quickly on a hot dish with a garnish of parsley.

TIMBALES DE MACARONI

Butter some small moulds about the size of a teacup, line them with well-boiled macaroni, round like a beehive; have ready veal and ham, chicken and tongue, or cold game, minced very fine, a little pepper, salt, cayenne, two eggs, and a cup full of cream. Mix all together and fill the moulds; boil for half an hour and turn them out, and serve with good brown gravy or with white sauce. Less cream may be used if the above quantity is thought too rich.

SAVORY RICE

Take some plainly boiled rice, put into a saucepan with a lump of butter; add as much tomato sauce as the rice will take up, and plenty of grated Parmesan cheese; mix well; and keep stirring on the fire till hot. Serve piled on the dish.

RICE CROQUETTES

Wash well one teacupful of rice; put it to boil in a pint of milk and the same of hot water, until quite tender, but dry. While hot, add a piece of butter the size of an egg, two tablespoonfuls of white sugar, two eggs, the juice and grated peel of one lemon; stir this up well. Have ready the yolks of two eggs, beaten on a plate, some fine cracker crumbs on another. Make up the rice with your hands in rolls about three inches long and two inches round; dip into the egg, then into the crumbs; fry them in hot lard to a light brown. Serve hot.

RIZ A LA TURQUE

Put into a saucepan six cupfuls of stock or broth into which you have previously dissolved a good allowance either of tomato paste, French tomato sauce, or the pulp of fresh tomatoes passed through a sieve; pepper and salt according to taste. When it boils, throw in for every cupful of stock half a cupful of fine rice, well washed and dried before the fire. Let the whole remain on the fire until the rice has absorbed all the stock, then melt a goodly piece of butter, and pour it over the rice. At the time of serving, and not before, stir lightly to separate the grains, but do this off the fire.

HOMINY

Take white corn if you can get it, none but plump corn. Shell it and boil in weak lye until the hull is broken. Then drain off the lye and rinse the corn in several waters (the old way is nine times, but six will do). Cover with plenty of water and return kettle to the stove and boil until tender, which usually takes almost the entire day. As the water boils away, add more (hot is better than cold).

GREEN CORN PUDDING

Grate the corn from four good-sized ears; add one pint of milk, two well-beaten eggs, a piece of butter the size of an egg, salt and pepper to taste. Stir three tablespoonfuls of flour in a little cold water, add it to the rest, beat all well together, and bake an hour.

CANNED CORN FRITTERS

Drain off the liquor from a can of corn, chop fine, add three beaten eggs, a small cup of milk, a tablespoonful of melted butter, two tablespoonfuls of flour, and a teaspoonful of baking powder. Season with pepper and salt. Fry by the spoonful on a griddle.

SCALLOPED TOMATOES

Pare and slice fine ripe tomatoes; put into a bake-dish with alternate layers of buttered bread crumbs; season each stratum of tomato with pepper and salt. Bake covered until very hot, then brown. The upper layer should be of crumbs.

STUFFED TOMATOES

Take a dozen firm, well-shaped tomatoes. Have a pound of cold roast beef, or the same of cold steak, or if you use raw meat it is just as good. Chop an onion with a tablespoonful of parsley; add two teaspoonfuls of salt and a saltspoonful of white pepper; pound up six soda crackers. Fry the onion thoroughly in a tablespoonful of butter, to which, when cooked, add the meat, which has also been divided; let it all cook thoroughly with the onion and parsley. Take the tomatoes, cut off the stem end, which you do not use, remove the inside of the tomato and add to the meat; then mix the meat, etc., with the pounded cracker, fill the tomatoes, which are to be placed on a bake-pan, and bake for one hour in a moderate oven.

STEWED POTATOES

This excellent way of cooking potatoes may seem so simple as to make any directions unnecessary. They are, however, so frequently done poorly that the dish itself has come to be lightly esteemed. Slice cold boiled potatoes until you have at least a quart. They must be cut evenly, but not too thinly if the potatoes are very mealy. Cover with nearly a quart of rich milk, and set over a slow fire. Sprinkle on some pepper and salt and a lump of butter. An open frying pan is best for the purpose. They should be at least fifteen minutes in coming to a boil, after which simmer slowly for from a half to three-quarters of an hour. Never let them boil rapidly, and do not stir them. If there is any danger of their sticking to the pan, grasp it by the handle and shake gently. If they become too dry add more milk. They are very nice for dinner with cold boiled mutton, or with broiled chicken, and for breakfast with salt mackerel, broiled or boiled. Children are very fond of potatoes prepared in this way, and they are healthful and nutritious.

POTATO SALAD

To one pint mashed potatoes (those left over from dinner are just right), add the smoothly rubbed yolks of three hard-boiled eggs, reserving the whites cut in transverse slices to garnish the dish. Slice one cucumber pickle, and add one teaspoonful ground mustard, pepper and salt to taste. Heat one teacup good vinegar, dissolving in it a lump of butter the size of a walnut. Pour the vinegar over the pickle and seasoning and add the mashed potatoes by degrees, rubbing and incorporating thoroughly. I think you will find it an agreeable addition to the table.

Another recipe for the same dish: Boil some Irish potatoes; when done, mash, and season with salt, pepper, and butter. Mince a large onion and three hard-boiled eggs, and mix thoroughly through the potatoes. Add a half cup of vinegar and one teaspoonful mustard.

POTATOES TOSSED IN BUTTER

Take some small new potatoes, lay them in salted water, rub off their skin with a coarse cloth, dry them, put them in a saucepan with plenty of butter. Keep tossing them now and then until they are quite done, which will be in about half an hour, when add a sprinkling of salt, and serve.

POTATO CAKES

Grate one teacup raw ham, mix with one quart mashed potatoes. Beat and stir into this two eggs; add pepper, salt, and a little mustard. Roll into balls and fry a light brown. Sage and sweet marjoram can be added, if liked.

POTATO SOUFFLES

Take some large potatoes, peel them, and cut them in slices rather less than one-quarter inch thick, dry them thoroughly with a cloth, and put them in the frying basket. Have ready two pans filled with boiling lard, plunge the basket into one of them, and keep shaking it. In two or three minutes lift up the basket and plunge it into the other pan; when the slices of potatoes swell out, drain them of all fat and serve. The secret of success consists of removing the basket from the first pan at the right time. The potatoes should not be allowed to color in it.

BAKED CABBAGE

Boil a firm, white cabbage for fifteen minutes in salted water, then change the water for more that is boiling, and boil until tender. Drain and set aside until cool, then chop fine. Butter a baking dish and lay in the chopped cabbage. Make a sauce in this way: Put a tablespoonful of butter in a pan; when it bubbles up well, stir in one tablespoonful of flour, and one-half pint of stock, and one-half pint of water, both boiling; stir until smooth, season with pepper and salt, and mix well with it four tablespoonfuls of grated cheese. Pour this over the cabbage, sprinkle rolled crackers over it, dot it with lumps of butter, and place in a quick oven for ten minutes. This is almost as good as the more aristocratic cauliflower when cooked in the same manner.

COLD SLAW

An excellent cold slaw is made by shredding a solid head of cabbage with a thin, sharp knife or slaw cutter, then placing the cut cabbage in your dish, pouring over it a dressing made by heating a pint of vinegar scalding hot, then beating into it quickly one beaten egg, with a lump of butter as large as a walnut, and a tablespoon of sugar. The cabbage should be thinly sprinkled with salt and pepper as it is put in the dish.

For hot slaw, prepare the same as for cold slaw, cook tender, and pour over the dressing, or merely season with vinegar before dishing up.

BOILED CAULIFLOWER

Pick off the outside leaves, cut the stalk close to the flowers, and lay the head in cold water for half an hour. Boil it in salted water until tender, and remove to a hot dish. Send to the table with drawn butter in a separate boat. The sauce Hollandaise is especially nice for cauliflower.

STEWED ONIONS

Wash, peel, and cut into slices six fine large onions, and put into a stewpan with one quart of cold water and one-half small teaspoonful of soda. When the water comes to a boil, pour off and set the onions back over the fire with one cup of boiling water, one and a half cups of sweet milk, a large tablespoonful of butter, one-half teaspoonful of sugar; season to taste and boil half an hour.

FRIED ONIONS

Peel, wash, and cut onions crossways so as to form undivided rings. Flour well and fry in drippings for about ten minutes. Drain, sprinkle with salt and pepper, and serve.

TO COOK SQUASH

The small scalloped squash should be boiled in salted water until you can pierce them easily with a fork. Then lay in a sieve to drain, and as soon and they are cool enough to handle, scrape off the skin, cut them open, take out the seeds and pulp, and return the pieces of squash to the saucepan. Mash smooth, season with pepper, salt, and butter, and serve.

The Boston and Hubbard varieties may be peeled, cut in pieces, and boiled until done. Then drain, mash, and season as before.

Another nice way of preparing squash for the table or for pie is to cut them in two, lay in a baking pan, and bake until done in a moderate oven. Cooked in this way, they will always be dry.

TO COOK EGG PLANT

Slice thin, peel, rub each piece with salt, and cover all with water, putting a weight on top to keep them under. Let them stand for two or three hours, then wipe the slices dry. Dip each one into beaten egg, then into rolled cracker crumbs, and fry in equal parts of very hot butter and fresh lard until they are well cooked through, and of a bright brown color.

VEGETABLE CURRY

Cut some onions in thin slices and fry them a good brown in butter. Add a breakfast cupful of milk, in which a tablespoonful of curry powder has been mixed; let all boil together for twenty minutes, stirring the whole time. Then add the vegetables previously parboiled, and let the whole simmer by the side of the fire for about an hour. Potatoes, peas, beans, carrots, and turnips can be used, but broad beans alone make a delicious curry.

BOSTON BAKED BEANS

Wash the required amount of beans, cover with cold water, and place on the back of the stove until the water becomes tepid, then add a small piece of baking soda and bring it to a boil. Drain and cover again with boiling water, letting them simmer until the skins burst. Then take a genuine bean pot, put in half the beans, next a nice piece of salt pork (about half a pound to a pint of beans), and then the remaining beans, with the liquor. Season with pepper, add a lump of butter, cover closely, and bake at an even temperature for five hours. Keep them covered with water for three hours, afterward allowing it to boil down. These may be baked in the afternoon, and remain in the oven all night, to reheat for breakfast.

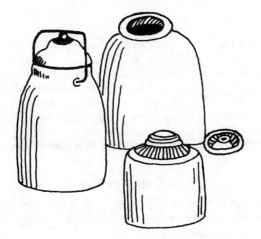

APPLE FRITTERS

Peel three large apples, core them and cut them across in slices rather less than half an inch thick. Put them in a flat dish with half a tumbler of brandy and strew plenty of powdered loaf sugar over them. Let them remain covered for a couple of hours, then take each piece separately, dip it in butter so that it is well covered with it, and fry a golden color in plenty of hot lard. Lay the fritters in front of the fire, and when all are done pile them up on a napkin, shake plenty of powdered loaf sugar over them, and serve.

APPLE COMPOTE

Peel, core, and halve six large apples, trimming them so as to get them all of a size. Drop them as they are done into cold water with the juice of a lemon squeezed into it, to prevent their turning brown. Have ready a strong syrup (made with a pound of sugar and one quart of water) boiling hot. Put the apples into this, with the thin rind of a lemon and two or three cloves. As soon as they are cooked (great care must be taken that they do not break) take them out and dispose them on a glass dish, concave side uppermost. Place a piece of currant jelly in the hollow of each apple, then well reduce the syrup, and, when cold, pour as much of it as is necessary under the apples.

STEWED PEARS

Cut a number of pears in halves, peel them, and trim them so as to get them all of a size. Put them into an enameled saucepan with just enough water to cover them and a good allowance of loaf sugar, the rind of a lemon, a few cloves, and sufficient prepared cochineal to give them a good color. Let them stew gently till quite done. Arrange them neatly on a dish, strain the syrup, let it reduce on the fire, and when cold pour it over the pears.

BANANA PUDDING

Slice the fruit in thin pieces, laying them in layers with a little butter and sugar sprinkled between each layer. Bake in a moderate oven.

FRUIT BISCUITS

Fruit biscuits, which are so relished by many as short cakes, may be prepared in this way: Make a crust as for biscuit, roll out a half-inch thick, cut in rounds or squares. After placing one layer of these on the tin, place another layer of the same size over them. Put in the oven and bake. When done, these layers are easily separated, and any kind of stewed, canned, or preserved fruit may be placed between them, and they are very convenient when one has not time to prepare pie.

SNOW CUSTARD

Half a box of gelatine, three eggs, one pint of milk, two cups of sugar, juice of two lemons. Soak the gelatine in a teacup of cold water one hour. When dissolved, add one pint of boiling water, and two-thirds of the sugar and lemon juice. Add to the whites of the eggs, whipped to a froth, then put it in the dish in which it is to be served, or in a mould. Make a custard of the milk, yolks of the eggs, remainder of the sugar and lemon juice, and just before serving, pour it round the mound of jelly.

ORANGE JELLY

Make a syrup with one pint of water and one pound of loaf sugar, boil it with the thin rind of four oranges and two lemons, skim it carefully, and add the juice of eight oranges. Let it boil about twenty minutes, skim, and add the juice of a lemon and either one pint of calvesfoot jelly or sixteen sheets of the best French gelatine dissolved in half a pint of water and clarified with whites of eggs. Peel a couple of sweet oranges, removing every particle of skin of both kinds, core them to get rid of the pips, and cut them in thin slices in such a way as to get rid of the pellicle round each quarter. Proceed to fill the mould, disposing pieces of oranges in it in a symmetrical fashion. When set, turn out the jelly in the usual way.

CORN STARCH BLANC MANGE

Four tablespoonfuls of corn starch, one quart of milk, one teaspoonful of butter. Dissolve the starch in some of the milk. Put into the remainder of the milk, one table-spoonful of sugar, a little salt, a piece of lemon rind or cinnamon stick, and heat up to near boiling. Then add the mixed corn starch, and boil (stirring it briskly) four minutes. Take out the rind, and pour into a mould or cup, and keep until cold. Serve with sauce or sugar and cream and preserved fruit.

BAKED PUDDING

Three tablespoons of corn starch, one quart of milk. Prepare and cook the same as for blanc mange. After it is cool, stir up with it, thoroughly, two or three eggs, well beaten, with four tablespoonfuls of sugar, flavor to taste, and bake half an hour.

RICE PUDDING

One and one-half cups of rice, one and one-fourth cup-fuls of sugar, two quarts of milk, one cupful of raisins, and salt to taste. Place all together in a pudding pan, and bake slowly until done, but do not let it bake too hard.

TAPIOCA PUDDING

Soak two-thirds of a cupful of tapioca over night in one quart of milk; then add three beaten eggs, five table-spoonfuls of sugar, butter the size of an egg, and one whole lemon, grated. Bake three-quarters of an hour. Serve with cream or milk.

POTATO PUDDING

Boil four large potatoes, and pass them through a sieve. Stir into them powdered loaf sugar to taste, and the yolks of two eggs. Add a few drops of essence of lemon, then the whites of the eggs whisked to a froth. Mix quickly and well, pour into a plain mould, buttered and bread-crumbed, and bake for twenty minutes in a quick oven.

SWEET POTATO PUDDING

Beat to a cream one pound of butter and one pound of sugar. Boil and mash fine two pounds of sweet potatoes, and beat them by degrees into the butter and sugar. Add five well-beaten eggs, a wineglass each of wine and brandy, and one of rose water, two teaspoons of mixed spices, and a half pint of cream. Bake in a crust.

POPCORN PUDDING

Soak two quarts of freshly popped corn in three pints of sweet milk over night. When ready to bake, add three well-beaten eggs, a little salt, and sugar to taste. Bake like a custard pudding.

BREAD AND BUTTER PUDDING

Cut thin slices of bread, and butter without the crust. Butter baking dish well. Wash currants, dry them, and put in first, also some candied lemon peel, cut up small. Strew sugar over it. Place over this the bread and butter in several layers; pour on some milk, and let it soak for a quarter of an hour. Now make a custard of two eggs, milk, white sugar, and flavor with nutmeg. Pour over and bake half an hour or more. This pudding, when turned out, has a pretty appearance.

DELICIOUS PUDDING

Take a deep pudding dish and butter it. Cover the bottom and sides with thin slices of bread, white or brown, then a layer of pared and cut apples or pears, or both, mixed with any other fruit you fancy. Then sprinkle some sugar on, then a layer of bread in slices or bits, then fruit, and so on until the dish is full. Lay thin slices of bread over; fill up with any fruit juice or, lacking this, water. Cover with a plate and bake in a slow oven four hours. Hot or cold, it is most delicious. Any sauce would spoil it.

MELANGE

Line a deep dish with pie crust and spread on a thin layer of tart applesauce, then a layer of buttered bread, on this another layer of apples. Bake until the crust is done. When done, spread on the whites of two eggs, beaten to a froth and sweetened, and brown slightly. Serve with pudding sauce of butter and sugar stirred to a cream, seasoned with lemon.

BAKED APPLE DUMPLINGS

One quart flour, two tablespoons lard (half butter is better), two cups of milk, one teaspoon soda dissolved in hot water, two teaspoons cream of tartar sifted into the dry flour, one teaspoon salt. Mix the shortening into the flour after you have sifted it and the cream of tartar together, put in the soda, and wet up quickly just thick enough to roll into a paste less than half an inch thick. Cut in squares and lay in the center of each a juicy, tart apple, pared and cored. Bring the corners of the squares together, and pinch slightly. Bake to a fine brown. Eat hot with rich, sweet sauce.

PUFF PASTE

Take equal quantities of flour and butter; before mixing, wash the butter thoroughly, then lay it in ice water. Take the flour, adding a teaspoonful of salt for each pound, and mix into a stiff, smooth paste, using ice water for mixing. Allow the dough to lie five minutes, then roll it out thin. Flatten the butter into a sheet to cover the center one-third of the dough, fold the top and bottom thirds of the dough over it, and roll the dough out again. Repeat the folding and rolling five times, leaving the paste about ten minutes each time. Keep the paste as cool as possible. It will be better if allowed to lie on ice several hours before baking. Bake in an oven as hot as for baking white bread.

FLAKY PIE CRUST

Best of flour, butter, salt water. Take as much flour as you need, dry it before the fire, and sift it, then mix it with water to form a stiff paste. Roll it out one way (from you), put on it small bits of butter, roll the sides together, and roll in the butter. Repeat this three times, and be careful to always roll the same way. If your butter is very salty, do not add any more.

LEMON PIE

One lemon, one tablespoonful of corn starch, one teaspoonful of butter, one cup of sugar, two eggs, and one cup hot water. Put the sugar and water together over the fire, and into them, while boiling, stir the corn starch previously dissolved in a little cold water. Stir in the grated rind of the lemon and the pulp cut very fine. Beat up the eggs, reserving the white of one, and stir them in. Bake in a plate lined with crust, in a quick oven. When done, spread over it the white of the egg previously beaten with sugar into a stiff froth, and return to the oven for a few moments.

CARROT PIE

Wash and scrape or peel the carrots and cut them crosswise into pieces about an inch long. Rinse them in clean water and stew them till soft; then mash them fine. A nice way is to pass them through a sieve or cullender. To one quart of sweet milk for a family pie, three eggs are enough. Stir in the stewed carrots with your milk and beaten-up eggs till it is as thick as you can stir round rapidly and easily. About one tablespoonful of fine flour may be added, but do not get it too thick. If the pie is wanted richer, make it thinner and add sweet cream or another egg or two, but even one egg to a quart of milk makes a good pie. Sweeten with molasses or sugar. If a fine flavor is wanted, two tablespoonfuls ground cinnamon may be added, also a little salt. Bake about an hour in deep plates or shallow dishes without an upper crust.

IRISH POTATO PIE

Parboil peeled potatoes, slice a layer into an uncooked crust. Mix one cup white sugar with one teaspoon cinnamon and one-fourth teaspoon nutmeg. Add half of sugar mixture to cover potatoes, and repeat. You may add a third layer of potatoes if desired, but then use another half-cup of sugar and seasonings in proportion. Cover with top crust. Start in a hot oven and bake until crust is brown and crisp. Should be drippy when cut.

CREAM TARTS

Make a short, sweetened pie crust, roll thin, and bake partly in sheets. Before it is done, take from the oven, cut in squares of four inches or so, take up two diagonal corners and pinch together, which makes them basket-shaped. Now fill with whipped cream or white of egg, or both, well sweetened and flavored, and return to the oven for a few minutes. Jelly, or chocolate, or cream filling, such as is used for cake, might also be used.

RHUBARB TARTS

Cut the stalks from the leaves and peel off the skin, and cut into small pieces. Wash and put into a saucepan to stew with no more water than that which adheres to them. Add sufficient sugar to make the sauce sweet enough and let it simmer slowly until thick. When done and cool, line patty pans with good stiff paste, put in the filling, and bake in a quick oven. Add any flavoring that suits the taste.

ORANGE TARTLETS

Make a short paste with one white and three yolks of eggs, an ounce of sugar, a little milk, an ounce of butter, a pinch of salt, and flour *quantum suff*. Work it lightly, roll it out to the thickness of a quarter of an inch, line some small patty pans with it, fill them with uncooked rice to keep their shape, and bake them in a moderate oven until done. Peel off the thin rind from a number of oranges, make a thick syrup by boiling some loaf sugar in a little water; let the orange rind infuse in this for a little time, but not boil in it. With a sharp knife remove from the oranges every vestige of any rind, core them as you would apples so as to get rid of the pips, cut them in half lengthwise, lay them in a tin, pour the syrup over them and put them in the oven to get quite warm. Empty the tartlets of rice, put a half orange into each, pour a little of the syrup over, and again put them in the oven to keep hot till the time of serving.

ECCLES CAKE

Make a rich and delicate puff paste; roll it out thin; cut it round, using a bowl for that purpose; sprinkle each round with nicely washed currants, a little sugar, chopped lemon (only a small quantity of lemon), and nutmeg. Wet the edges well, then place another round of paste on the top, pressing the edges neatly together; put in a hot oven and bake quickly.

GINGER CAKES

Two cups of molasses, one and a half cups of butter, two cups of sour milk, one teaspoon of ground ginger, and one heaping teaspoon of soda. Mash the soda, then mix all the ingredients together in a suitable pan, and stir in flour as long as you can with a spoon; then take the hand and work in more flour, just so you can roll them by using flour dusting pretty freely. After that roll out thin, cut, and lay upon floured tins. Then mix one teaspoonful of molasses and two of water, and with a bit of cloth wet over the top of the cakes; this removes the dry flour, causes them to take a nice brown, and keeps them moist. Put into a quick oven, and ten minutes will bake them if the oven is sufficiently hot.

COCOANUT DROPS

Cream one pound of sugar with three-quarters of a pound butter. Add the beaten yolks of four eggs, and stir in two grated cocoanuts and the whites of the eggs beaten to a stiff froth, alternately with four tablespoonfuls of sifted flour. Drop on buttered tins and bake. The prepared or desiccated cocoanut may be used, but the cakes are much inferior to those made with freshly grated cocoanut.

ALMOND MACCAROONS

Scald twelve pounds of almonds, take off the skins, and throw into cold water until all are done. Then pound them with one tablespoonful essence of lemon to a smooth paste, and add equal weight of powdered loaf sugar and the whites of three eggs. Work the paste well with the back of a spoon, then dip fingers into cold water and make into little balls and lay on white paper. Dip the hand into cold water and pass over each one. Bake in a cool oven three-quarters of an hour.

LADY FINGERS

Rub half a pound of butter into a pound of flour, add half a pound of sugar, grate in the rind of two lemons, and squeeze in the juice of one. Then add three eggs, make into a roll the size of the middle finger (it will spread in the oven to a thin cake), and bake. Dip in chocolate icing.

SOFT GINGERBREAD

Half a cup of sugar, half a cup of molasses, one cup of sour milk, one cup of shortening, two eggs, and one heaping teaspoon of soda, and flour. Do not make too stiff —you can try a small one first. Stir the soda in the molasses till it foams, and beat eggs and sugar together.

SWEET CORN CAKE

Take three eggs; beat light; add one cup sour milk or cream, one cup of flour, then one cup and a half of sugar and a half cup of butter or lard, corn meal to make a middling stiff batter, nutmeg or any kind of spice to suit taste, and one teaspoonful soda. One cup of raisins added is nice, and baking powder can be used if preferred to soda. This cake is nice for lunch, to eat with coffee or tea, or berries and cream.

UNION CAKE

One cup of butter, two of sugar, one of sweet milk, three of flour, one-half of corn starch; four eggs; two teaspoonfuls of lemon extract, one-third of soda, and one of cream of tartar. Take one half of this dough, spice it to taste, and bake it in patty tins. The other half may be baked in a loaf, making a variety for your cake basket.

SOUR MILK CAKE

One pint of sour milk, two cups of sugar, two cups of chopped raisins, one-half cup of butter, one dessert spoonful of soda, all kinds of spice. Stir in flour till quite thick and bake.

FARMER'S CAKE

One egg and the yolk of another, one cup of sugar, a lump of butter as large as a hen's egg, half a nutmeg, grated, one cup of sour cream, two-thirds of a teaspoon of soda, one heaping cup of flour. Beat the eggs, sugar, and butter together, then add cream, soda, nutmeg, and flour last. If you wish it extra nice, put in the whites of two eggs, whisked to a froth, and use white pulverized sugar and one teaspoon of essence of lemon; leave out the nutmeg.

RAISIN DELICATE CAKE

Two cups of granulated sugar, good half-cup of butter, whites of six eggs beaten to a froth, three-fourths of a cup of sweet milk, three cups of flour, one cup of seeded raisins, cut fine, two teaspoonfuls of yeast [baking] powder, and two teaspoonfuls of lemon extract. Cream the butter, then the sugar with the butter; stir in the milk, then part of the flour—one cupful should be reserved for the raisins—then the whites, and lastly, the fruit. After adding the flour, whisk in the whites and fruit as quickly as consistent with thorough mixing, and bake.

The Sod-House Period   71

RIBBON CAKE

Two cups of sugar, three eggs, two-thirds cup of butter, one cup of milk, three cups of flour, one teaspoonful of cream of tartar, salt and flavoring. Mix this as any cake, and divide it, baking half in an oblong pan. To the remainder add one tablespoonful of molasses, a cup of raisins, a quarter pound of sliced citron, spices, and a little flour. Bake in same shaped pan as the light cake, and while warm, put them together with jelly or jam between. Cut in squares when cold; is very nice.

SILVER OR BRIDE'S CAKE

The whites of sixteen eggs beaten to a froth; stir into them one pound of pulverized loaf sugar. Cream together three-quarters of a pound of butter and one light pound of sifted flour; add all together; use no spices; flavor with lemon, vanilla, or rose. Almonds blanched and powdered are an improvement. Use rose water with the almonds to prevent them from oiling.

SPONGE CAKE

Take four eggs, two coffee cups of sugar, two coffee cups of flour, two teaspoons of cream of tartar, one teaspoon of soda, two-thirds of a cup of boiling water, and lemon to flavor. Beat egg yolks and sugar well together; add the egg whites, whisked to a froth, alternately with the flour, through which the soda and cream of tartar are sifted. Add the water and flavoring last. Bake in shallow tin in a well-heated oven. This, though apparently thin, will be a delightful cake.

JELLY CAKE

Ten eggs, the weight of the eggs in sugar, the weight of six eggs in flour, one fresh lemon (half the grated rind and all of the juice). Carefully separate the eggs, beat the yolks, sugar, and lemon together until very light; then the whites to a stiff froth. Mix thoroughly and add the flour, beating it in lightly. Bake in a square or oblong pan quickly without drying. Turn the cake out onto a clean cloth, roll it up, and let it remain until cold. Success will depend upon proper baking and being expeditious in spreading and rolling. When cold, unroll and spread with jelly or chocolate or cocoanut icing and roll up again. Not everyone has the conveniences for weighting; in that case, let them try any sponge cake recipe they may have.

DUTCH APPLE CAKE

Two cups of flour, three teaspoonfuls baking powder, one tablespoonful sugar, one-fourth teaspoonful salt, four tablespoonfuls fat, one egg, one cup of milk. Mix all dry ingredients and cut in the fat. Add the egg and milk, pour into a shallow greased pan and cover with topping made as follows. Cook one and one-half cups sliced apples in one-half cup of water, slowly, for five minutes. Add one teaspoonful ground cinnamon mixed with one-half cup sugar and two tablespoonfuls butter and cook two minutes more. Cool and spread on soft dough and bake twenty minutes in moderate oven.

PRUNE CAKE

One and one-fourth cups sugar; three-fourths cup butter; one egg; one cup cooked, stoned prunes; one cup juice from the prunes, with one teaspoonful soda dissolved in it; one teaspoonful ground cinnamon; one-fourth teaspoonful ground nutmeg; one-fourth teaspoonful ground cloves; one-fourth teaspoonful salt; two teaspoonfuls baking powder; three to four cups flour; one cup nut meats. Bake in moderate oven about an hour.

ROYAL FRUIT CAKE

Five cups of flour, five eggs, one and one-half cups of sugar, one cup of molasses, one and one-half cups of butter, one teaspoon of saleratus, one-half cup of milk, two pounds of chopped raisins, three pounds of currants, two teaspoons of allspice, two tablespoons of cinnamon, two teaspoons of cloves. Mix well and bake in slow oven.

ICING FOR CAKES

Beat the whites of two eggs to a high froth; then add to them a quarter of a pound of white sugar ground fine like flour. Flavor with lemon extract or vanilla. Beat until it is very light and white; the longer it is beaten the firmer it will become. No more sugar must be added to make it so. Beat the frosting until it can be spread smoothly on the cake. This quantity will ice quite a large cake, top and sides.

CHOCOLATE ICING

Put into a saucepan one-half pound of powdered loaf sugar, two ounces of grated chocolate, and about a gill of water; stir on the fire until the mixture assumes the consistency of a thick, smooth cream.

CHOCOLATE CREAMS

Mix two ounces of Bermuda arrowroot smoothly with one and a half gills of water; add twelve ounces pulverized sugar, and boil rapidly from eight to ten minutes, stirring continually. Remove it from the fire and stir till a little cool; flavor with vanilla or rose; continue stirring till it creams, then roll into little balls. Melt some chocolate over steam (add no water) and when the cream balls are cold, roll them in it one by one and lay on a buttered slab to cool. The creams may be varied by dividing the cream into three parts, adding grated cocoanut to one, chopped almonds to another, and pistachios to the third.

RHUBARB JAM

To six pounds of rhubarb add six pounds of lump sugar and six large lemons; cut the rhubarb into small pieces about the size of a walnut; then the lemons should be sliced, and the peel cut very fine. Put the fruit (taking out the pips from the lemons) all into a large bowl, then cover it with the sugar broken small. Let it stand twenty-four hours, after which boil it slowly for about three-quarters of an hour, taking care it does not stick to the pan, also not to stir so much as to break the pieces of rhubarb, as the beauty of it is in being whole. If the fruit is gathered in dry weather, it will keep any length of time and be delicious.

PEACH, PEAR, OR QUINCE BUTTER

To thirteen pounds of fruit add one pint vinegar and four pounds of sugar. Boil till as thick as required.

YELLOW TOMATO PRESERVES

Use small pear tomatoes; do not peel them. Put in almost as much sugar as you have tomatoes and add sliced lemon—one lemon will flavor two gallons. Cook until thick.

For tomato butter do the same, only rub fruit through a cullender first.

PLUM SAUCE

Use small sour plums; four pounds of sugar and one and a half pints of vinegar to seven pounds of fruit. Tie up one ounce each of whole cloves and stick cinnamon in muslin bags and boil in the vinegar for ten minutes. Add the sugar and fruit and simmer slowly for several hours until it becomes very thick. Stir frequently to prevent burning. This is an excellent sauce for cold meat or roast ducks or game of any kind, and will keep for several years.

SWEET TOMATO PICKLE

Seven pounds ripe tomatoes, peeled and sliced; three and a half pounds sugar; one ounce mace and cinnamon, mixed; one ounce cloves; one quart vinegar. The spice must all be ground. Mix all together and boil one hour.

TO PICKLE RIPE CUCUMBERS

Cut them in slices, lay them in weak salt and water over night, then rinse in cold water and boil in a syrup of a quart of vinegar, three pounds of brown sugar, and spices; boil until clear.

PICKLED PURPLE CABBAGE

Cabbage, salt, vinegar, mace and cloves, whole white peppers, sugar, celery seed. Wash the cabbage and cut in quarters. Lay it in a wooden tray and sprinkle thickly with salt, set in the cellar till the next day, drain off the brine, wipe dry, and lay it in the sun two hours; then cover with cold vinegar and let it stand twelve hours. Then prepare the pickle by taking vinegar enough to cover it, add a cup of sugar to each gallon of vinegar, and a teaspoonful of celery seed to each pint. The spices should be boiled in the vinegar and poured hot on the cabbage. Keep in a cool place. Ready for use in six weeks.

PRESERVED WATERMELON RIND

Pare off the green skin and cut into strips or fanciful shapes. Line a kettle with vine leaves, fill with the rind, and scatter a little pulverized alum over each layer. Cover with vine leaves, three deep, and pour on enough water to wet that. Cover closely and allow them to steam for three hours, without letting the water boil. Take out the rind, which will be of a fine green color, and throw it into cold water. Let it remain in soak, changing the water every hour, for four hours. Use four lemons, a quarter of a pound of ginger, and six pounds of sugar for every six pounds of the rind. Wrap the ginger root in a muslin bag and boil in three pints of water until the water is highly flavored; remove the ginger, put in the sugar, and boil and skim until no more scum arises. Put in the pieces of rind and the juice of the lemons, simmer gently for an hour; take out the rind and lay upon dishes in the sun until firm and almost cool, put back into the syrup, simmer for half an hour, spread out again, and when firm pack into bowls and pour over the boiling syrup.

CUCUMBER CATSUP

Take one peck of full-grown cucumbers; remove the rind and cut them down lengthwise, then into thin pieces; strew one-half pint of salt on them; let them stand five or six hours; then put them in a sieve to drain quite dry. Peel and slice twelve large silver-skinned onions and put into strong vinegar. Add for seasoning one tablespoon of cayenne, one-fourth cup of sweet oil, one-fourth cup of Madeira wine, and a few blades of mace. Fill wide-mouthed glass bottles with the cucumbers, and pour the vinegar over. If you have a few pods of the minature variety of red peppers to use instead of the pulverized cayenne, they give the sauce an ornamental appearance.

TO PRESERVE ORANGE JUICE

Squeeze out a pint of juice from the best oranges to be procured, strain it through fine muslin, and let it simmer gently for twenty minutes with three-quarters of a pound of loaf sugar. When cold, put it into small bottles.

LEMONADE

Upon the very thin rind and juice of four good-sized lemons put sugar to your taste, and three pints of boiling water. The lemonade should be made thirty-six or forty-eight hours before using it. Leave the peel in one day. Strain before using.

GINGER BEER

One pound of loaf sugar, one ounce of cream of tartar, one and a half ounces of best white ginger (bruised), one gallon of boiling water. Pour the water upon these ingredients, and let it stand till the next morning, when it may be bottled. It is better to strain it through muslin when bottled.

Immigrant Cookery

T HE COOKING of Nebraska's foreign-born settlers gave a dis-
tinctive and cosmopolitan aspect to the state's cuisine. More
than a quarter of a century after she took up residence in the
East, Willa Cather wrote, "I could name a dozen Bohemian
towns in Nebraska where one used to be able to go into a bakery
and buy better pastry than is to be had anywhere except in the
best pastry shops of Prague or Vienna. The American lard pie
never corrupted the Czech." In her Nebraska novel *My
Ántonia*, the American-born narrator is surprised at the Bohemian custom of cooking cucumbers in milk, and Ántonia's son
makes a point of his mother's spiced plums, used in kolaches
("Americans don't have those").

Mari Sandoz's writing tell us much about the German-Swiss
food of her father, Old Jules's, family in the Sandhills. In "The
New Frontier Woman" she describes how her mother prepared
"the world's most divine concoction—Swiss plum pie":

> . . . perhaps she will make you a pie or two or even three—for
> one piece, she is certain, would be an aggravation. Gently she
> tests the plums between her fingers, choosing only the firmest,
> to halve and pit and lay in ring after ring like little saucers into
> crust-lined tins. Then sugar and enough of the custard, her own
> recipe, to cover the plums to dark submerged circles. She dots

the top with thick sweet cream, dusts it with nutmeg, or if you insist—but it is a serious sacrilege—with cinnamon, and slips them into her Nile-green range, gleaming as a rare piece of porcelain and heated to the exact degree with corncobs.

In *Old Jules*, Mari's mother fixes *Weinschnitte* for supper: "[She] dipped the slices of bread lightly in wild grape wine and into egg batter and fried them brown in butter. While still hot she sprinkled them with cinnamon and sugar and piled them high on a big platter." Caroline Sandoz Pifer, Mari's sister, recalls gathering mushrooms—sometimes as large as a dinner plate—which were boiled in seasoned water and fried lightly in butter. Immigrants from Central Europe also dried mushrooms and ground them to a powder for use in soups.

Thüna, a form of creamed spinach or other greens, was popular in the Sandoz household. Mari described it in a letter to a friend:

Spinach creamed (or any one of a lot of other greens: young radish, turnip, or that butteriest of all greens, the universal weed called lambs quarter), is an old Swiss dish, and while I almost never bother to cook for anyone anymore, when I do, Sandoz Green Thüna (traditional in our family of horticulturists, at least by avocation) are usually part of the menu. These call for light bread sponge, or light roll dough. I learned to make Thüna on my fifth birthday, which happened to be baking day. The recipe goes like this:

Cook greens not too done, drain, chop fine on wooden chopping board with old butcher knife in a merry rat-tat-tat that children love to do for you. Then turn into skillet generously buttered and already browned a little. Add thick sweet cream, salt, pepper, sprinkle with a little flour and stir. Should be gruely in consistency after a little simmering. Set aside and cool.

Roll out light bread sponge thin, cut into strips about 6–7 inches long, two inches wide, line tin such as used for corn sticks, fill with creamed spinach, dot with little dabs of sour cream, thick, to make nice brown blisters, bake and serve while warm, to be picked up and eaten like corn sticks.

If there is no local aversion, a bit of finely chopped schnittlauch [chives] may be added to simmering spinach, or a clove of garlic speared on a fork stirred around during the simmering, then lifted out.

The creamed spinach baked in a sponge-lined piepan or large

Immigrant Cookery 79

baking dish, the top spoked with bacon, makes a nice luncheon dish on baking day, etc.

To top off a dinner party, Mari recommended, in lieu of dessert, *küchli*, served with tart jam or red wine late in the evening.

KÜCHLI

Three eggs, six tablespoonfuls farm cream, one heaping tablespoonful sugar, three to three and one-half cups flour. Mix eggs, cream, and sugar together in a bowl. Work in all the flour you can, finally kneading dough vigorously with knuckles. When the consistency of firm noodle dough, roll paper-thin, cut into diamond pieces 4, 5 inches long, put aside a while if convenient. Fry lightly in deep hot fat, lift between long forks, dust with a bit of sugar. Pile the fragile pillows carefully on a large tray.

Although each national group had its distinct foods, some dishes were shared by several, for example, the fruit soup of the Scandinavians and the Germans, and the potato dumplings which were common to Middle Europeans in general. The ethnic designations in the following recipes indicate the origin of the donor of the particular recipe but do not necessarily mean that the dish was unique to that nationality.

SAUERKRAUT (German)

Use wooden tub or stone jar. Slice the cabbage fine by means of a slaw cutter or sharp knife. Place a layer of clean cabbage leaves on the bottom of the container. Sprinkle over them a small handful of salt and put in a layer of cut cabbage about six inches in depth. Sprinkle over the cabbage a small handful of salt, and by means of a wooden beetle or the end of a round stick of hard wood, pound the cabbage until juice appears. (Do not pound or salt too much.) Now add another small handful of salt, then pound, and continue this process until the container is nearly full. Cover the top over with clean cabbage leaves, and lay over these several thicknesses of cheese cloth. Place a clean board or plates over this and weight down with a clean stone or jars filled with sand. Let stand in a warm place for three or four weeks until it ferments. After forty-eight hours if a brine has not formed, add a little salt water (suitable to taste) to cover the cabbage. After two days more, add more salt water if necessary, until brine forms over the board cover and a scum appears. Remove the cloth cover, taking the scum with it, rinse thoroughly in cold water, wring dry, and return to its place. Continue to do this every few days until it ceases to ferment. This will require four or five weeks. It is then ready to use and may be stored in any cool, dark place.

To keep what is left of sauerkraut after winter use through the summer, squeeze out the brine through a cheese cloth. Select an earthenware jar, sprinkle the bottom with salt, and pack the sauerkraut in this. Make a brine by dissolving one tablespoon of salt to a quart of cold water. Bring to a boil over a slow fire, removing the scum as it rises. Set aside to cool and pour over the sauerkraut. Lay over the top several thicknesses of cheese cloth, and tie over the jar a piece of cotton batting. This will keep until the hottest days of summer.

KRAUT BERUCK (German)

Melt some butter in a skillet and add chopped onion, stirring until transparent. Add finely chopped cabbage and cover to steam until done. Brown some ground beef and add to the cabbage and onion, seasoning with salt and pepper to taste. Roll out bread dough, cut in squares, place a large spoonful of beef and cabbage mixture on each, fold dough over, and pinch edges together. Let rise and bake.

PFEFFERNÜSSE (German)

Two cups dark syrup or molasses, one-half teaspoon black pepper, one-half teaspoon nutmeg, one-half teaspoon ginger, one-half teaspoon cloves, one tablespoon anise seed, two cups sugar, one cup black coffee, one teaspoon soda, one teaspoon baking powder, two cups butter, one teaspoon salt. Mix all the ingredients together, adding flour to make a stiff dough. Roll into long rolls about an inch in diameter and cut with a sharp knife about one-half inch thick. Bake in a moderate oven ten to twelve minutes, until done. These are a traditional Christmas treat and will keep indefinitely.

SCHMIERKÄSE PIE (German)

Prepare a single pie crust and fill with the following: Make a custard with milk and eggs (flour may be used for thickening if eggs are not available). Sweeten to taste with sugar or sorghum. Add a cup of cottage cheese and a half a cup of raisins, chopped. Season with nutmeg and bake in a slow oven until done (knife inserted in the center comes out clean).

GERMAN DOUGHNUTS (KREBBEL)

Four cups flour, three eggs, one-half cup sugar, two cups milk, two teaspoons baking powder, two teaspoons salt. Mix same as other doughnuts; roll flat, cut in five-inch squares, and make a slash in the center. Fry in hot lard, and roll the cooked doughnuts in sugar to coat.

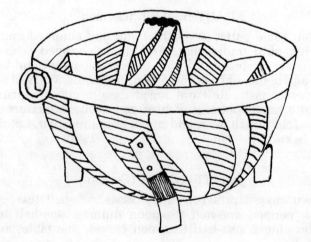

RODON KUCHEN (German)

Two cups sponge, three-fourths cup butter, one-half cup sugar, four eggs, one cup raisins, one-half cup almonds chopped fine, little grated rind of lemon. Mix butter and sugar well, add the eggs well beaten, then add sponge, beat for twenty minutes, then add flour gradually to make a stiff batter, let rise in a warm place. After it is well risen add raisins, almonds, and lemon rind; beat well again, put in a pan (you must have Turks-head pan made of copper) to rise; bake from three-quarters to one hour.

FRUIT SOUP (Scandinavian, German-Russian)

Take dried fruits, such as apricots, prunes, peaches, pears, raisins, and currants; cook slowly together in enough water to cover well; then add a little soaked tapioca to thicken and sugar to taste. May be boiled with a stick of cinnamon and sliced lemon for seasoning.

LUTFISK (Swedish)

Drop pieces of fish into salty water and keep at boiling point for about fifteen minutes, but do not boil hard. Cool and pick out all the bones and skin. Serve with a rich cream sauce made with one-fourth cup butter, one-fourth cup flour, two cups rich milk, and salt and pepper to taste. Some like a little mustard in the sauce also.

LEFSE (Swedish)

Boil enough potatoes to make about four cups mashed, and mash fine. Add half a cup of cream, a third a cup of butter, and a teaspoon of salt; beat until light, and let cool. Then add two cups of flour and one teaspoon sugar. Pinch off pieces of dough; roll out as for piecrust, as thin as possible; and bake on top of stove or pancake griddle until light brown, turning frequently to prevent scorching. Use moderate heat. When baked, place between clean cloths to keep from drying out. This is often eaten with lutfisk.

SWEDISH HEAD CHEESE

Three pounds of pork shank, one pound veal shank, two pounds of beef shank, two pig's feet. Boil all together; and when cool, slice in cubes, put in a cloth, and season with salt and pepper. Pour the hot liquid in which it cooked over it and let it stand in a pan, with a heavy weight on it. When it is pressed, take it out of the cloth and put in a crock of brine.

SWEDISH MEAT BALLS (KJÖTTBOLLAR)

One and one-half pounds ground lean pork, one-half pound ground beef, one egg, slightly beaten, one-half cup bread crumbs soaked in milk, one cup fresh mashed potatoes, salt and pepper to taste, and a pinch of allspice. Mix all the ingredients, roll into balls, and fry. When brown, add a little water, cover, and put on a slow fire to simmer for ten or fifteen minutes.

KOLDAIMA (Swedish)

Take one medium head of solid cabbage; boil until half done, take up and let drain until cold. Grind beef or veal fine and season with salt and pepper, a little butter, a little cream, and a pinch of sugar. Work together until well mixed, then cut off the large leaves of the cabbage. Put a spoonful of the mixture on each leaf, shape into oblong rolls, folding the cabbage leaves over, and fasten with toothpicks. Brown in butter and boil slowly in just enough water to cover about one and a half hours. May be served with brown gravy.

SWEDISH STUFFING

Mix together one-half cup raisins and two and one-half quarts of dry bread (half rye and half white) broken into small cubes. Pour enough boiling water over to moisten bread slightly. Then add one small onion, grated fine, two slightly beaten eggs, salt, pepper, three teaspoonfuls ground sage, one teaspoonful cinnamon, one-half teaspoonful cloves, and one-half teaspoonful allspice. Add enough milk to moisten the ingredients thoroughly and mix well. Stuff and bake fowl as usual.

SWEDISH COFFEE BREAD

One and one-half quarts of milk; one cup bread starter, three cups sugar, one-half pound of butter, one teaspoonful ground cardamom seed, flour to make a soft dough, one teaspoon salt. Mix flour, warm milk, one cup of sugar, and starter, and set to rise. When light, add rest of sugar, cardamom seed, butter, and flour, and work it well. Let it rise again before forming into loaves or cakes.

SWEDISH FLATBREAD

Combine two cups white flour or one cup each white and graham flour, one teaspoon salt, and two tablespoons butter. Add boiling water to make a stiff dough, stirring continuously, and cool. Roll out thin on a board sprinkled with corn meal and bake on top of stove, turning so as to brown evenly. Finish drying in oven for crisp flatbread.

DANISH SPICED MEAT ROLL

Clean a beef flank, cutting away all the bones, and spread it out on a board. If too big, cut into desired sizes. Sprinkle with salt, pepper, and a layer of sliced onions. Then roll up tight, sew with a strong thread, and leave it in a strong salt brine for three days. Before cooking, tie well with string to keep it from falling apart. Place in a pan with water to cover and cook until tender. When done, put away into a heavy press for a day. Then remove string and slice in thin slices.

DANISH MEAT BALLS

One pound ground beef, one pound pork sausage, one cup rich milk, five tablespoons flour, salt and pepper to taste, one large onion, minced. Mix meat, flour, salt, pepper, and onion together, working in the milk a little at a time until the mixture slips off the spoon. Fry meat balls in hot lard over a slow fire, browning on all sides. When done, make a milk gravy and serve with potatoes or other vegetables.

AEBLESKIVER (Danish)

Three eggs, three teaspoonfuls sugar, one teaspoonful salt, two cups buttermilk, two cups flour, one teaspoonful soda, one teaspoonful baking powder. Beat egg yolks and add sugar, salt, and milk, then soda and baking powder, sifted with the flour. Last add the stiffly beaten egg whites. Cook until bubbly; turn carefully, using an ice pick or two-prong fork; and finish cooking other side. Serve with sugar, syrup, or jelly. These require a special iron pan with rounded cups, which should be filled about half full.

KLEJNER CAKES (Danish)

One pint sweet cream, one tablespoon sugar, two eggs, flour. Mix cream, eggs, and sugar. Work in as much flour as it takes to slip dough off the hands. Roll dough out until the thickness of the back of a knife. Cut in strips five inches long and two inches wide. With a knife, make a slit in the middle and stick one end through the slit, so that the cake is twisted in the middle. Cook in hot grease until light brown (as for doughnuts).

BOHEMIAN PRESSED BLOOD SAUSAGE

Boil head, snout, ears, tongue, and a piece of meat from the neck. When done, cool and cut into dice. Add rendered lard and cracklings, fresh blood (beaten to prevent clotting), salt, pepper, ginger, and allspice fried in lard. Fill a cleansed pork stomach with this and boil an hour. When it can be pierced with a toothpick and no blood runs out, it is done. Place in a press in a warm place and put a weight on it. It is served with vinegar and pepper or vinegar and onion.

KOLACHES (Czech)

Scald one pint of milk, let cool to lukewarm. Dissolve one and one-half cakes compressed yeast in one-fourth cup lukewarm water to which one teaspoon of sugar has been added. Let rise while milk cools. Add dissolved yeast to cooled milk and make a sponge. Let rise until light. Cream together one cup sugar and one cup butter. Add three egg yolks and two whole eggs, well beaten, and two teaspoons salt. Add to the sponge and mix well. Stir in flour enough to handle well. Let rise until light and roll out to one-half inch thickness. Cut with a biscuit cutter. Make a depression in the center and fill. Let rise and bake in a quick oven. Any of the following fillings can be used:

Fruit filling: Mash stewed prunes. Add sugar and cinnamon to taste, and sprinkle with coconut or chopped nuts. Apricots, peaches, apples, or any canned fruit may also be used.

Poppy seed filling: Grind poppy seed and boil it in just enough water to keep moist. Then add sugar, cinnamon, and maple syrup to taste; raisins; and three or four gingersnaps, ground.

Cottage cheese filling: Combine grated rind of lemon, one-half cup sugar, one tablespoon cream, two egg yolks, and one pint of dry cottage cheese.

APPLE STRUDEL (Czech)

One-half cup butter; three cups flour; one-half teaspoonful salt; three-fourths cup warm water; one slightly

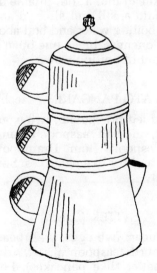

beaten egg; eight cups sliced apples; three-fourths cup butter, melted; one cup sugar; one teaspoonful ground cinnamon; two cups dry bread crumbs; one cup chopped walnuts (optional); one cup raisins (softened in boiling water and drained). Cut butter into flour and salt as for pie crust. Combine water and egg and add to butter and flour mixture, stirring well. Turn out on lightly floured board, knead five minutes, and divide dough in half. Cover and let stand thirty minutes. Cover board with cloth and roll dough very thin. Brush with butter and half of sugar combined with cinnamon. Combine bread crumbs with two tablespoonfuls melted butter. Arrange half the apples on dough, top with bread crumbs, and alternate bread crumbs with half of walnuts and raisins. Pick up cloth slowly and evenly raise it, making dough roll into a tight roll. Seal edges (removing cloth) and place on large, shallow buttered pan, curving slightly. Brush top with milk. Repeat with other half of dough and filling. Bake in moderate oven about fifty minutes.

POTATO DUMPLINGS (Czech)

Two cups mashed potatoes, cooled; add two well-beaten eggs and blend thoroughly. Add enough flour with a little salt in to knead into a soft, pliable dough that will not stick. Make into a roll and slice in about three-inch pieces. Drop into boiling water and boil about twelve minutes. To test for doneness, break one open with two forks after you take it out of boiling water.

POTATO PANCAKES (Czech)

Two cups shredded raw potato; two eggs, beaten; one-half teaspoon salt; one-half teaspoon baking powder; one and one-half tablespoons flour. Drain potatoes; mix in other ingredients and fry like pancakes. Serve with syrup or any kind of jelly.

SVITEK (Czech)

One-half cup sugar; five eggs, well beaten; one quart sweet milk; one-fourth teaspoonful salt. Add enough flour to make a thin batter (like pancakes). Pour batter into well-greased baking pan. Drop fresh stoned cherries (about one quart or more if preferred) into batter and sprinkle with one-half cup more sugar. Bake in moderate oven thirty minutes. Other fruit may be substituted.

PIGS' FEET (Polish)

Wash and cut in half four pigs' feet and two pork shanks. Put into a large pot, cover with water, bring to a boil, and skim. Add one onion (cooked in butter), one stalk of celery, chopped, a few sprigs parsley, one clove of garlic, five peppercorns, five allspice, and four bay leaves. Simmer four or five hours, then cool and remove bones and spice. Add salt to taste and a tablespoon of vinegar. Pour meat and broth into a pan, set in a cool place until it jells, and remove fat from the top.

CZARNINA (DUCK BLOOD SOUP) (Polish)

Put vinegar into a glass or crockery bowl (not metal). Kill duck and drain blood into the bowl, stirring constantly. Simmer the duck trimmings and blood with one and a half pounds of spareribs, one stalk of celery, a few sprigs parsley, one onion, four whole allspice, four whole cloves, salt to taste, and three peppercorns. When nearly done, add about ten dried prunes, some dried apples or pears, and three handfuls of cherries or raisins. Before serving, stir in two tablespoons of flour, one cup cream, two teaspoons honey, and one-half cup vinegar. Pig's blood can be used instead of duck's.

EGG NOODLES (MACARONI) (Polish)

Put one cup of flour on a dusted board and form into a hill with a hole in the center. Drop in one egg and one-fourth teaspoon salt. Mix and add one-half eggshell of water. Knead until dough is smooth, then roll thin and put on a floured cloth to dry for several hours. Sprinkle dough lightly with flour and roll tight. Cut the rolled dough into thin noodles, toss to separate, and dry. Boil in salted water until noodles rise to the top, drain, and rinse in cold water. Store what is not used immediately uncooked in a jar.

CHEESE CAKES (Polish)

Force two cups dry cottage cheese through cheese cloth. Add two eggs, two tablespoons cream, and one-fourth cup sugar and beat thoroughly; then add one-fourth cup raisins and one cup flour. Roll into balls, make an indentation in the center, and fry in butter. Fill the center with fruit or sour cream and sprinkle with cinnamon.

PIEROGI (Polish)

Three cups flour; three eggs, beaten; one teaspoonful salt; one-half cup milk; cottage cheese sweetened with a little sugar and seasoned with salt. Mix flour, eggs, salt, milk, and a little water if needed to make the consistency of noodle dough. Knead well, roll out, and cut into three- or four-inch circles. Fill one side of each with about two tablespoonfuls cottage cheese. Fold over other side, seal or crimp like pie crust, and drop one or two at a time into boiling water. Keep turning them so that they don't stick to the bottom of the pan. Boil five or six minutes, or until they rise, then fry lightly on each side in butter and onions.

PRUNE SOUP (Polish)

Two cups of dried prunes, a handful of raisins; cook in water to cover well. Season with a pinch of salt and add a tablespoonful of sugar or to taste. When done, add dumplings. Serve with a half cupful of sweet cream over it.

VARONIKAS (Jewish)

One cup left-over mashed potatoes, two eggs, four tablespoonfuls matzoth flour, chopped left-over veal, salt and pepper. Add beaten eggs, flour, and seasonings to potatoes and mix thoroughly. Shape into balls, scoop a hole in the center of each, and fill with chopped meat. Cover the opening with the potato mixture, roll again, dip in matzoth meal and egg, and fry in chicken fat until golden brown.

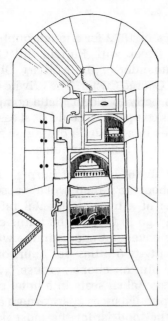

Dining En Route

THE PASSAGE of the Homestead Act, the completion of the Union Pacific across Nebraska in 1868, and the construction of the Burlington, which entered the state in 1870, were major factors in drawing settlers—and along with the homeseekers, the railroads brought tourists. "From earliest times, even before the completion of its tracks to their eventual meeting with the Central Pacific at Promontory, Utah, in 1869, the Union Pacific had been a favorite with western excursionists, the pioneer railroad that opened limitless vistas to a nation on the march toward continental destinies," writes the noted railroad historian Lucius Beebe. "As early as 1867 when its railhead was still in mid-Nebraska and the Hell-on-Wheels that accompanied it was making night hideous far short of unborn Cheyenne, an excursion was arranged out of New York to ride the steamcars as far as the hundredth meridian at Platte City."

In the decades before the turn of the century thousands of Englishmen—literary figures like Robert Louis Stevenson, Oscar Wilde, and Rudyard Kipling; nobility; military officers; clergymen; and other lesser lights—visited the American West. The Grand Duke Alexis of Russia, "in perhaps the most commodious and perfect manner in which any one ever traveled by

Dining En Route   91

rail," came to Nebraska in 1872 for a much publicized buffalo hunt on Red Willow Creek with Buffalo Bill Cody, General Philip Sheridan, commander of the Military Division of the Missouri, and General George Custer. The private train that carried the Grand Duke's party to North Platte comprised "a day car, in which he and his companions could sit at ease, read, write, or amuse themselves as in a parlor; a dining or hotel car, into which they walked to breakfast or dinner; and a sleeping car."

The same article in an 1872 issue of *Harper's New Monthly Magazine* that described the Grand Duke's accommodations extolled the pleasures of a transcontinental railroad trip for Americans. From Chicago to Omaha the trains carried dining cars, where "you may have your choice in the wilderness, eating at the rate of twenty-two miles per hour, of buffalo, elk, antelope, beef-steak, mutton-chops, grouse." But "beyond Omaha, unless you have taken seats in a hotel car, you eat at stations placed at proper distances apart, where abundant provision is made, and the food is, for the most part, both well cooked and well served. . . . Sufficient time is allowed—from thirty to thirty-five minutes—to eat; the conductor tells you beforehand that a bell will be rung five minutes before the train starts, and we always found him obliging enough to look in and tell the ladies to take their time, as he would not leave them."

Most of the English visitors disagreed with that writer's evaluation of the restaurants, although those who had traveled in the West earlier by stage admitted that they were an improvement over the stage stops. They found the meals, which regularly cost a dollar, heavy, badly prepared, and unattractively served, and the time allowed for eating inadequate. Robert G. Athearn, in his lively book *Westward the Briton*, quotes one Englishman who expressed a typical British view:

Let me here remark, with all possible courtesy, that the American on his travels is the most reprehensible eater I have ever seen. In the first place, the knives are purposely made blunt—the back and front of the blade being often of the same "sharpness"—to enable him to eat gravy with it. The result is that the fork (which *ought* to be used simply to hold the meat steady on the plate while being cut with the knife) has to be used with great force to wrench off fragments of food. The object of

Nebraska Pioneer Cookbook

the two instruments is thus materially abused, for he holds the
meat down with the knife and tears it to bits with his fork! ...
This abuse of knife and fork then necessitates an extraordinary
amount of elbow-room, for in forcing apart a tough slice of beef
the elbows have to stick out as square as possible, and the conse-
quence is, as the proprietor of a hotel told me, only four Americans can eat in a space in which six Englishmen will dine com-
fortably.

Dining En Route 93

Like his fellow countrymen, he was appalled at the westerner's eating habits—"He dabs his knife into the gravy of the steak, picks up with his fork a piece of bacon, and while the one is going up to his mouth, the other is reaching out for something else"—and concluded of the railroad eateries, "I, as a traveller, see no reason whatever, no necessity, for their being kept alive at a cost of so much suffering to the company's customers."

Those who could afford to travel first class took accommodations in a hotel car, "one of the most ingenious as well as one of the most convenient of all modern arrangements for travel." It was described by the *Harper's* correspondent as "containing two drawing-rooms, . . . one state-room having two double berths, and six open sections of two double berths each (in all twenty-two berths), and having also, in one end, a kitchen fully equipped with every thing necessary for cooking and serving meals."

It can seat forty persons at the tables; it contains not only a kitchen—which is a marvel of compactness, having a sink, with hot and cold water faucets, and every "modern convenience" —but a wine closet, a china closet, a linen closet, and provision lockers so spacious as to contain supplies for thirty people all the way from Chicago to the Pacific if necessary.

No price schedule was included for the hotel cars, in which meals were ordered and served at the traveler's convenience, but the menu for the dining cars between Chicago and Omaha offered a surprisingly good variety:

BROILED.

Porter-house Steak	$0 75	Spring Chicken	1 00
Do., with Mushrooms .	1 00	Do., half.	75
Mutton-Chops, plain . .	50	Breakfast Bacon	40
Do., with Tomato Sauce	75	Broiled Ham	40
Veal Cutlets, breaded .	50	Lamb Chops, plain	50

COLD DISHES.

Sliced Boiled Tongue .	40	Sardines	40
Do., Ham	40	Pickled Lobster	40
Pressed Corned Beef . .	50	Spiced Oysters	40

Nebraska Pioneer Cookbook

OYSTERS.

Raw	50	Stew	50
Fancy Roast	75	Fried	60

EGGS.

Boiled Eggs	25	Shirred Eggs	30
Fried Eggs	25	Omelet, plain	30
Poached Eggs	25	Do., with Rum	40
Scrambled Eggs	30	Do., and Ham	40

VEGETABLES.

Green Corn	10	New Boiled Potatoes	10
New Green Pease	10	Fried Potatoes	10
Stewed New Potatoes	10		

RELISHES.

Chowchow	10	Worcestersh'e Sauce	
Mixed Pickles	10	Walnut Catsup	
Queen's Olives	15	Tomato Catsup	
Horse-Radish		French Mustard	

PRESERVED FRUITS.

Peaches	25	Apricots	25
Prunes	25	Damsons	25
Blackberries	25	Cherries	25
Pine-Apples	25		

BREAD.

Dry Toast	10	Hot Biscuit	10
Milk Toast	25	Corn Bread	
Buttered Toast	25	French Loaf	
Albert Biscuit	10	Boston Brown Bread	
Dipped Toast	15		

BREAKFAST WINES.—Claret and Sauterne.
CHAMPAGNE WINES.—Heidsick and Krug.

French Coffee, English Breakfast Tea, and Chocolate	15
French Coffee, Tea, Chocolate, without an order	25

The Burlington also furnished dining-car service at an early date. A reporter for the *Railway World* in 1876 wrote that the line had constructed several dining-room cars "of a very superior quality" furnished "in the finest style of art." "It begins to look," he continued, "as though dining by rail would soon supersede the old way of stopping at hotels along the road."

While economy-minded passengers frequently carried lunch baskets, for dining-car patrons an increasingly elaborate menu and the addition of a massive silver service—including the traditional duck press as well as individual chafing dishes, egg boilers, toasters, and coffee percolators—made dining en route more and more luxurious.

BAKED HAM, UNION PACIFIC STYLE

Select a "ready-to-eat" smoked ham and have your butcher remove the hock and hip bone. Also have him trim the ham and score the fat side for baking. Place the trimmed and scored ham in a baking pan and cover well with the following, thoroughly mixed: one cup light brown sugar, one teaspoon ground cinnamon, one-fourth teaspoon ground allspice, one-half cup flour. Rub the mixture into the scored fat side of the ham with the hands. After the mixture is applied to the ham, neatly arrange six thin slices of canned pineapple on top, securing them to the ham by sticking several whole cloves through each slice. This will hold the pineapple in place during the baking. Pour over the ham the juice from the can of pineapple or other fruit juices available, together with an equal quantity of water. Bake in a moderate oven for one hour, basting frequently and adding water as needed to prevent baking pan from becoming dry and scorching the drippings. When done, the ham should be golden brown and well glazed. Prepare sauce from the drippings in pan, seasoning it with a little sherry wine, currant jelly, chopped orange with peel, or steamed raisins as desired. Serve with slices of pineapple or browned sweet potatoes.

UNION PACIFIC FRENCH TOAST

For one portion, use two slices of table bread three-fourths of an inch thick and trimmed free of crust. Cut diagonally, making four triangular pieces. Dip in mixture of two eggs and one basting spoonful (or about two table-spoonsful) of cream well beaten. Fry until golden brown in hot clarified butter and lard (using half of each) in a shallow pan. Serve hot and well drained. The top may be sprinkled with powdered sugar if desired.

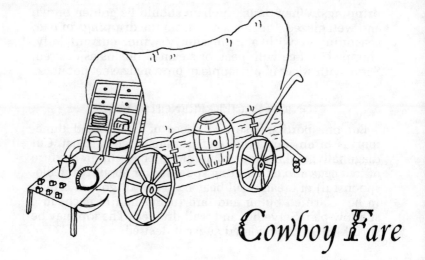

Cowboy Fare

FOLLOWING CLOSE on the extension of rail service through the state and the extermination of the bison, the range cattle industry solidly established itself in the 1870s as a mainstay of Nebraska's economy. During the colorful era of the open range, one of the most important and best-paid members of a ranch outfit was the cook, for he had to be a master at preparing hearty, satisfying meals in limited time under extremes of weather and terrain.

Cowboy historian Ramon Adams, in his essay "Cookie," identifies the "five pillars" of cowboy fare as coffee, beans, meat, sourdoughs, and stew. These were supplemented by dry foods which could be carried in the chuck wagon: dried fruit; rice, which might be cooked with raisins for "spotted pup"; and perhaps canned vegetables such as corn and tomatoes.

The coffee pot was always on the fire. "Most range cooks prided themselves on their coffee," Ramon Adams writes.

> Cookie knew his charges wanted it strong and black. He used lots of coffee in proportion to the water, let it boil hard for a time and served it fresh. Just before it was ready, he added a pinch of salt and a dash of cold water to settle the grounds. He had no percolators. His recipe for making coffee suitable to drink was "take one pound of coffee, wet it good with water, boil it over a

fire for thirty minutes, pitch in a horseshoe. If it sinks, put in more coffee."

Adams quotes a story about the proverbial rule that prevailed in a cow camp when there was no regular cook: "When anybody complains about the chuck, they have to do the cooking. One cowboy broke open a biscuit and he says, 'They are burnt on the bottom and top and raw in the middle and salty as hell, but shore fine. Just the way I like them.' "

A. B. Snyder, whose reminiscences of cowboy life have been recorded by his daughter Nellie Snyder Yost in *Pinnacle Jake*, recalls that once when the cook quit he substituted for about ten days until another could be hired. "There was no kicking about the grub," he adds, "for I never shed my six-shooter while I was cooking." On taking over as cook, Pinnacle Jake recounts,

I didn't know how the grub was loaded in the wagon, so I just about had to unload the whole wagon to find what I needed to get dinner with. . . . I loaded up again, to suit myself, but when I got through I had a hundred-pound box of dried apples left over. The wagon was plumb full and there was no place to put the apples, unless I unloaded and loaded up again different, to make a place for the case of apples. I sure wasn't going to do that, and I didn't like dried apples much, anyway.

I didn't want to leave the box setting there on the prairie though, so I looked for a place to get rid of it. None of the boys had come into camp yet, and there wasn't anyone around but me, so I picked up the box and went over to the creek bank. The creek was almost dry, except in some places where the water stood in "potholes." The potholes were generally pretty deep, so I dumped the apples, box and all, into one of them, and it sunk to the bottom, out of sight.

Returning to the area a couple of weeks later, Doc, the roundup boss,

happened to ride up on the creek bank to unsaddle his horse. All of a sudden he yelled, "What the hell is that in th' creek?" All the boys went over to see what Doc meant. I knew what he saw, all right, but I went over too, to see what those dried apples looked like by then.

They had swelled and swelled, until the pothole was full of

apples. There was no sign of the box, just a haystack-sized pile of dried apples. Doc and the boys tried to figger out what the mess was. They guessed different things, and I guessed maybe it was an old excelsior mattress that somebody had throwed in there. Nobody made any better guess, and I never did tell anybody what it really was.

Yeast, or "light," bread sometimes replaced the standard sourdough biscuit, baked in big Dutch ovens with a layer of hot coals underneath and on top. "Baking light bread on a roundup was quite a trick," according to Pinnacle Jake.

The dough had to be mixed and set to raise the night before, then carried along in the pans when the wagon moved on, next morning. The cook had to get his wagon camped in time to get his fire going, his dutch ovens heated and his bread baked by noon, if he could. If he couldn't get it done for dinner then he mixed up a batch of baking powder biscuits for that meal, and went ahead and baked the bread for supper.

When he was pinch hitting as cook, Pinnacle Jake quickly became an expert on labor-saving devices:

I was pretty good at stirring up baking powder biscuits without dirtying any pans. I'd just open up the flour sack (in those days flour came in a fifty-pound cloth bag); make a hole in the flour, right in the sack; put in some baking powder, salt, and warm lard; and pour in some water. When I had enough flour mixed in with the other stuff to make a dough, I lifted the wad out of the sack and shaped up my biscuits. Quick and easy.

Nebraska Pioneer Cookbook

Beef was the cowboy's meat, and he ate every part of the animal that could be made edible. "Son-of-a-bitch stew," roundup fare par excellence, gave "cookie" a chance to express his culinary creativity. Ramon Adams tells how it was made.

The one ingredient which gave this stew its bad name among the uninitiated was the word "marrow gut." This is no "gut" at all, but a long tube connecting the two stomachs of young cud-chewing animals. It is good only when the calf is still nursing, being then tender and full of a substance which resembles marrow. Hence the name. Through this, the partially digested milk passes. This is why calves not completely weaned are selected for this stew. The marrowlike substance is left in when cooking the stew and is what gives it its delightful flavor.

I could give you at least a dozen recipes for this dish, if I had the space. Each would be a little different. Where one would use kidneys, another would not. One liked using the spleen, another preferred leaving it out. Some liked onions, others a dash of chili pepper. Here is a sample recipe:

½ the heart	All the butcher's steak (the
½ the spleen	strips of lean meat on the
¼ the liver	inner side of the ribs), or an
All the tongue	equal amount of tenderloin
All the sweetbreads	2 cups of melted leaf fat
Marrow gut (about 3 feet)	One set of brains

After the calf was killed and while the meat was still warm, the heart, liver, tongue, marrow gut, some pieces of tenderloin, or butcher's steak, sweetbreads and the brains were taken to be prepared. The cook cut the fat into small chunks, put them into the pot. While this fat was being melted he cut the heart into small cubes, adding it first because it was tougher. The tongue was also skinned and cubed, then added, thus giving the two toughest ingredients longer cooking time. While these were cooking, the cook cut the tenderloin, sweetbreads and liver into similar pieces, using the liver sparingly so as not to make the stew bitter. To all this was added the marrow gut after being cut into rings, or inch long pieces. Cover all this with lukewarm water, adding more from time to time.

The ingredients were added slowly, a handful at a time, the whole being slowly stirred after each addition. During this time the brains were cleaned of blood and membranes, then cooked separately, some cooks adding a little flour to make them thicker. When they became beady they were added to the stew, this being the last ingredient added except salt and pepper to taste, or a little onion if desired.

A favorite meal of the Snyder family on their McPherson County ranch in the years before World War I was their "bread 'n meat" supper. "We had these only in the wintertime when it was cold enough to freeze our home-butchered beef rock-hard," writes Mrs. Yost.

Mother would have baked up a big batch of "starter" bread and Dad would cut a huge platterful of paper-thin slices of meat from the round of a hind quarter. A bowlful of melted home-churned butter stood ready on the back of the big kitchen range.

Two big iron skillets, hot enough to wilt a poker, were lightly greased with a chunk of tallow and the thin slices of meat dropped in, quickly turned, then lifted out. We all stood round the stove (no one ever sat down to eat a bread 'n meat supper), holding our slices of bread slathered with melted butter. Mother forked the smoking meat onto our bread and we went at it, slice after slice. The gods never tasted anything so good.

Pinnacle Jake's wife, Grace Snyder, kept her best recipes—for cream puffs, White Cliff cake, and many others—in a leather-bound pocket-size account book which Pinnacle Jake brought home from a cattle-shipping trip to Omaha. Among them was "Ice Cream Like You Buy," an interesting switch today, when homemade ice cream is an unsurpassable treat.

———

ICE CREAM LIKE YOU BUY

Three quarts milk, one quart cream, three cups sugar, one ounce gelatin dissolved in a little warm milk, six egg whites. Scald one pint of the milk in a double boiler, add the gelatin and sugar and add to the remainder of the milk. Flavor to taste and add the beaten egg whites. Stir in the cream and freeze.

———

Buffalo Bill Cody, although he is best remembered as a scout and showman, was part owner of a ranching operation on the

Dismal River in the late seventies and early eighties. In her history of the Nebraska Stock Growers Association, *Call of the Range*, Nellie Snyder Yost describes him as "mostly a silent partner," but he usually showed up about roundup time with a wagonload of whiskey and cigars—"antidotes against snake bite and other accidents." On one occasion, she writes, some neighboring ranchers gave a dinner for him because "nothing was too good for Colonel Cody." "After the soup course came a big kettle of boiled beans." Everything went well until several of the guests passed their plates back to the host, serving from the big kettle at the head of the table. "He was getting pretty well to the bottom of the pot when he got hold of something that would not 'cut up.' Asking the cook . . . to bring him a fork, he snagged up the dirtiest, greasiest old dish rag any of them had ever seen."

Residents of North Platte, where Cody built his imposing home, Scout's Rest Ranch, in 1886, went all out on a "Welcome Home" dinner in his honor that year: the menu, starting with oysters and running to nearly forty items, listed among other things cold roast ham with champagne sauce, four salads, four varieties of bread, ambrosia, ice cream, fresh fruits, assorted nuts and layer raisins, five kinds of cake, and a good selection of wines, including the best champagne and brandy.

The Age of Elegance

THE SODBUSTER's frontier would last, at least in parts of the state, until the turn of the century and many Nebraska families would continue to live largely on cornmeal mush and sowbelly. But for the towns and cities, the 1880s were boom times economically and, by effect, gastronomically: Omaha's population quadrupled during the decade, while Lincoln, a contemporary journalist rhapsodized, "like a mountain stream, bounding free from its frozen embrace," sprang "into national fame and great prosperity." By "great prosperity" was meant the installation of running water, electricity, and telephones; and by the end of the decade these conveniences were helping to lighten the housewife's chores in both cities. Although foods were still prepared largely from scratch, cookery took on a new sophistication as the range of available commodities widened and as spirits were removed from the medicine cabinet to the pantry. The bride who brought to Nebraska the handwritten books from which these recipes were taken might well have prepared any of them.

Nebraska Pioneer Cookbook

BLACK BEAN SOUP

First make a stock by boiling any cold meat or bones you may have in about three quarts of water reduced to about one half. Let it stand over night, and the next day take off the grease. Over night soak one pint or one and a half of black beans, after washing them well. Boil them in two quarts of fresh water, throwing away that in which they were soaked all night. Press them through a wire sieve, pour the whole into a pot with the stock previously prepared, and season it like turtle soup, with one glass of wine, yolks of eggs, and forcemeat balls, slices of lemon, and a heaped teaspoonful of spices.

This is very good as a simple soup, by adding vegetables, leaving out the rich seasoning.

FORCEMEAT BALLS

Scrape fine enough raw lean veal or chicken to make one-half pound. Soak two ounces of bread (free of crust) in milk; when soft, pour it in a clean towel and squeeze dry; add two ounces butter, the scraped meat, and the yolks of two eggs. Pound the whole smooth, and force through a rather coarse sieve. Season with salt, pepper, and nutmeg. Form into almond-shaped balls between two teaspoons and cook about ten minutes in stock that must only simmer.

CHICKEN CHEESE

Prepare a chicken to boil. Boil till tender in as little water as possible. Take out the chicken; remove all the bones, fat, and gristle. Boil the liquor down to one pint, dissolve one-half box gelatine in as little water as possible, and add to it. Season with salt and pepper. Cut the chicken about as fine as for salad, put in a dish, pour the liquor over it, and set away to cool (it will have to stand till the next day). Cut in thin slices and garnish the dish with hard-boiled eggs or parsley. This is about right for a three-pound chicken and will make enough for six persons.

ROASTED OYSTERS ON TOAST

Eighteen large oysters, or thirty small ones, one tea-spoonful flour, one tablespoonful butter, one-half cup cream, salt and pepper. Have three slices toast buttered and on hot plate. Put butter in small sauce pan and when hot add dry flour, stir until smooth but not brown, then add cream and let boil once. Put oysters into their own liquor in hot oven for three minutes, then add them to the cream. Season and pour over the toast. Garnish the dish with thin slices of lemon and serve very hot.

NUN'S PUFFS

Boil one pint of milk; add one-half pound butter. Stir into these three-fourths pound of flour and let it cool. Then add nine eggs, the yolks and whites to be beaten separately, the whites to be added last. Fill your tins half full to bake, and sprinkle sugar over them to serve for tea.

CRULLERS

Boil one pint of new milk and melt in it one-fourth pound of butter; beat two eggs with one pound of sugar, and pour the boiling milk on them, stirring well all the time. When it is nearly cold, stir in half a teacup of yeast, half a teaspoonful of salt, and flour enough to make it a stiff batter. When this is quite light, knead in flour enough to make a soft dough; one nutmeg, grated; and a little mace. Let it rise again till it is very light; roll it out thin; cut it in shapes; and fry them in hot lard. Dust over them while hot, pounded cinnamon and loaf sugar.

CALF'S FOOT JELLY

A set of calf's feet; boil them in four quarts of water until reduced to two. They should be simmered, not boiled. Set the jelly away after being strained until the next day, when the grease must be taken off carefully, and the jelly boiled with the juice and rind of three lemons, one pint of wine, a little cinnamon, a pint of sugar, and the whites and shells of four eggs for twenty minutes. Then pour it into the jelly strainer and allow to drip without distur-bance.

WHIPPED JELLY WITH FRUITS

Prepare two cupfuls of preserved fruits; keep the cherries whole, but cut the others into dice. Moisten all with sherry. Prepare a quart of wine jelly, set on a basin of ice, then whip gently with egg whisk, adding the juice of two lemons. When it begins to set and is quite frothy but not too much, stir in fruits and place in mould on ice.

HUNTERS' PUDDING

Mix one pound of suet; one pound of flour; one pound of currants; one pound of raisins, stoned and a little cut; the rind of half a lemon, shredded as fine as possible; six Jamaica peppers (allspice), in fine powder; four eggs; a glass of brandy; a little salt; and as little milk as will make it of a proper consistence. Boil in a floured cloth, or a melon mould, eight or nine hours. Serve it with sweet sauce. A spoonful of peach water may be added for a change of flavor.

This pudding will keep after it is boiled, six months, if kept tied up in the same cloth and hung up folded in a sheet of cap paper to preserve it from dust, being first cold. When to be used, it must boil a full hour.

WINE CREAM SAUCE FOR PUDDING

Take a piece of butter the size of an egg, as much powdered or white sugar as you can braid into it, a little juice or rind of lemon, and glass of wine. When well beaten together, pour on the mixture a cup of boiling cream (or milk) and boil all up once.

FLUMMERY

Lay sponge cake in a deep dish. Pour on wine or rose water to moisten it. Make a boiled custard of yolks of eggs, milk, and sugar, and pour on the cake when cool. Beat the whites to a stiff froth and pour over the whole.

MARMALADE ROLL

One quart prepared flour, one tablespoonful of lard, two ounces of butter, one pint of milk, or enough for a soft dough. Rub the lard into the flour, wet with the milk, and roll very thin. Baste with the melted butter and sprinkle with flour lightly. Fold up and lay in a cold place for an hour. Roll out a quarter of an inch thick and spread with a cup of marmalade. Roll up and lay in pan with the joined edge downward. Bake three-quarters of an hour. Wash over with white of egg beaten with a little sugar just before done. Serve hot with liquid sauce.

FROZEN PUDDING

One quart of milk, four eggs, four cups sugar; make a soft custard. Dissolve two ounces of chocolate in the milk. Add to the custard one pint of good cream and the whipped whites of five eggs, and freeze. When stiff, stir in four ounces of raisins, three ounces of currants, and two ounces of citron cut fine and soaked in two glasses of sherry wine; also one-half pound Spanish chestnuts. Let it stand to stiffen. Serves twenty persons.

ROMAN PUNCH

Mix juice and grated rind of four lemons, four cups sugar, one quart water; strain. Freeze like ice cream. When ready to take out dasher, add one cup wine or spirits. Enough for twelve.

TRANSPARENT MARMALADE

Take some Sicily oranges, cut in quarters, take out the pulp, and clean it of seeds and skin. Put the peel in a little salt and water to soak over night. Pour off the water the next morning and boil in a good quantity of spring water till tender. Cut in shreds and add the pulp. To every pint add one pound of sugar and boil them together for twenty minutes. If it is not clear, simmer for some minutes longer, stirring all the time. When cold turn in jelly glasses.

SWEET PICKLED PEARS

One quart cider vinegar, three pounds brown sugar, one ounce whole spice tied in a muslin bag—cloves, allspice, and a little stick of cinnamon if you like it. Boil up once, then put in your pears, whole but peeled, and boil till tender. Place in a crock and when all are done, pour the liquor over them. This quantity will do about one-half peck, but if not quite enough to cover them, boil up a little more sugar and vinegar and put the spice bag at the top of the crock. If you prefer to use glass jars, throw away the spice bag, as they will be sufficiently spiced.

GLACE NUTS

Have ready walnuts or almonds laid on a buttered tin. Dissolve one cup sugar in one-half cup water. Let it boil, not stirring, until it hardens in water. Take out a spoonful at a time and pour over nuts, or dip the nuts in the syrup.

Hired girls were a standard fixture in the homes of business and professional men; in fact, going into domestic service was one of the few ways in which a country girl—particularly the daughter of immigrants like Ántonia in Willa Cather's novel—might find new opportunity and escape the drudgery of the farm. Annie Pavelka, the prototype for Ántonia, worked for the Miner family of Red Cloud; and like the fictional Ántonia, she baked hickory nut cakes for the young son.

HICKORY NUT CAKE

One and one-half cups sugar, one-half cup butter, two cups flour, two teaspoons baking powder, two-thirds cup water, one teaspoon vanilla, four egg whites, two-thirds cup chopped nuts. Cream sugar and butter together till fluffy. Sift together flour and baking powder and add alternately to creamed mixture with the water. Add vanilla and fold in stiffly beaten egg whites. Add nut meats and bake in a greased loaf pan or two layer pans in a moderate oven, fifty to fifty-five minutes for a loaf, twenty-five to thirty minutes for layers. Frost with boiled icing or serve with whipped cream.

Bess Streeter Aldrich, who lived nearly all of her adult life in Elmwood, sympathetically portrayed Nebraska small-town life in numerous novels and short stories. She considered herself a plain cook, writes her daughter, Mrs. Milton Beechner of Lincoln—"but I would add she was a good cook, as attested by the fact that my brothers and I always politely requested servings of our mother's food at all community or church dinners. She was well known for her luscious Lady Baltimore cakes, and her salads served from the gold rimmed Haviland china dish with the pink roses always seemed special." Bess Streeter Aldrich's family was particularly fond of her meat loaf and pumpkin pie; here are her recipes.

MEAT LOAF

One and one-half pounds ground round steak; one pound ground pork; one and one-half cup cracker crumbs; onion; salt; pepper; sage; two eggs, beaten. Mix meat, eggs, cracker crumbs, and chopped onion and seasonings to taste, and moisten with milk (should be quite moist). Shape into two loaves, put in lightly greased pans, place strips of pimiento across the top, cover pans, and bake in moderate oven for one and a half hours.

PUMPKIN PIE

One cup mashed pumpkin; one egg, beaten; two-thirds cup sugar; one cup milk; one teaspoonful flour; one-half teaspoonful ginger; one-half teaspoonful cinnamon; one-third teaspoonful cloves; one-third teaspoonful nutmeg; dash of salt. Mix ingredients and pour into unbaked pie shell. Bake at hot temperature for ten minutes and then moderately slow for about forty-five minutes, or until set.

The decade before the turn of the century saw the publication of cookbooks which would become standard authorities in kitchens across the nation. At the same time, women's church groups and aid societies by the dozens compiled and sold collections of their member's favorite recipes, occasionally interspersed with housekeeping hints and menus. A selection from Nebraska examples gives us a good idea of what the town and city families of the nineties were eating.

GOOD COFFEE

There are four essentials to good coffee: the best coffee, an egg, cream, and a *clean* coffee-pot. The coffee-pot should be emptied, washed, scalded, and dried every time it is used, just the same as other utensils. Coffee for two: three tablespoons best Java and Mocha. Mix with it thoroughly half an egg, then three tablespoons of cold water. Put the mixture into the coffee-pot, pour over it a little more than a quart of boiling water. Let it come to a boil and set it where it will boil very gently for fifteen minutes.

CHOCOLATE

Two teaspoons of grated Walter Baker & Co.'s chocolate to each cup; use milk and water in equal parts. Boil chocolate and water for ten minutes; heat milk in double boiler, but do not allow to boil. Sweeten chocolate and water slightly; add hot milk. Serve in cups with tablespoon of whipped cream.

The Age of Elegance   111

Bills of Fare for One Week.

BREAKFASTS.

SUNDAY.

Fruit.

Cracked Wheat and Cream.   French Fried Potatoes.

Broiled Oysters.

Rolls, Chocolate, and Coffee.

MONDAY.

Oat Meal and Cream.

Ham and Eggs.   Buckwheat or Wheat Cakes.

Coffee.

TUESDAY.

Fruit.

Graham Gems with Honey or Preserves.

Liver and Bacon.   Coffee.   French Fried Potatoes.

WEDNESDAY.

Cracked Wheat and Cream.

Eggs sur le Plat.   Thanksgiving Hash.

Muffins.   Maple Syrup.

Coffee.

THURSDAY.

Bananas with Lemon.

Codfish Balls.   Fried Potatoes.   Cream Biscuit.

Doughnuts.   Peach Preserves.

Coffee.

FRIDAY.

Oatmeal and Cream.

Bacon and Fried Apples.   Omelet.   Pancakes.

Coffee.

SATURDAY.

Oranges.

Broiled Beef Steak.   French Fried Potatoes.

Waffles.   Apple Jelly.

Coffee.

Nebraska Pioneer Cookbook

CREAM BISCUIT

Sift together two or three times one quart of flour and two heaping teaspoonfuls of baking powder, work in one tablespoonful of butter or lard and half a teaspoonful of salt, add one teacupful of cream, and beat to a soft dough. Roll to the thickness of three-fourths of an inch, cut out, and bake immediately.

GEMS

Two cups of flour, two eggs, two tablespoonfuls sugar, two cups sweet milk, two teaspoonfuls baking powder, two of melted butter. Bake in gem pans.

WAFFLES

Two cups flour, two cups milk, three eggs, two large tablespoons butter, two large tablespoons sugar. Beat the yolks, add the milk and butter melted, then the flour and one teaspoon salt; beat light; add the whites beaten stiff.

CREAM TOAST

Brown bread nicely on both sides. Let one pint of sweet cream come to a boil, add one tablespoonful of butter and a little salt, pour over toast and serve at once.

EGGS SUR LE PLAT

Beat two eggs separately, spread upon the platter, then drop as many eggs upon this as are required at the meal. Season with salt and pepper, sprinkle over with cracker crumbs, and place in a hot oven for a few minutes, when it is ready for the table.

SCRAMBLED EGGS

Melt one ounce of butter in a clean pan and break into it four fresh eggs, seasoning these with pepper, salt, and a very little nutmeg. Stir it continually for about three minutes, till it begins to set, then turn it into a hot dish, squeeze a few drops of lemon juice over it and serve very hot. This is a useful dish and can be varied almost indefinitely. Truffles, sliced and cooked for a few minutes in a little sherry; asparagus points or green peas, freshly boiled; shrimps, etc., tossed in a little butter and a very few drops of wine, can all be added to eggs cooked in this way. Scrambled eggs can be served in little cases of fried bread, or else halve some tomatoes, remove the pips and some of the flesh, put in a lump of butter with a little white pepper, and cook in oven till done but quite firm and shapely. Fill up the center with the scrambled eggs and serve.

BAKED EGGS

Delicious. Twelve eggs; boil hard, cut in two, take the yolks and mash fine. Add a large spoonful butter, one cup powdered crackers, one and one-half cups milk; season with pepper and salt; put the whites in a baking dish; pour this mixture over and bake fifteen minutes.

THANKSGIVING HASH

Take a dish suitable for the table, place a layer of bread crumbs in the bottom, then a layer of chopped turkey, next a layer of oysters, so on until the dish is filled. Pour over one pint of cream sauce, bake quickly for twenty minutes.

CODFISH BALLS

Boil potatoes and mash. Pick out codfish very fine and pour over it boiling water. Let stand until soft, then add potatoes, having one-half as much fish as potato, one egg well beaten, two tablespoonfuls cream, a little pepper, salt, and butter. Form into balls and fry before the mixture gets cold.

BANANAS WITH LEMON

Slice three or four ripe bananas in a dish and squeeze over them the juice of a good-sized lemon, then put over this a gill of ice water and half a cup of granulated sugar. Stand where it will get good and cold, and after half an hour it will be ready to serve. The lemons take away the naturally insipid taste and are healthy.

Bills of Fare for One Week.

DINNERS.

SUNDAY.

Roast Turkey.   Vegetable Soup.   Sweet Potatoes.
French Peas.   Stuffed Tomatoes.
Cream Slaw.   Celery.   Pickled Peaches.
English Plum Pudding.
Fruit.   Nuts.   Coffee.

MONDAY.

Broiled Beef Steak.   Tomato Soup.   Baked Potatoes.
Corn.   Celery.
Sliced Oranges.   Tea or Coffee.   Cake.

TUESDAY.

Bouillon and Celery.
Roast Leg of Mutton, Currant Jelly.
Lettuce.   Peas.   Boiled Potatoes.
Suet Pudding with Foaming Sauce.
Coffee.

WEDNESDAY.

Celery Soup.
Roast Chicken, Spiced Gooseberries.
Mashed Potatoes.   Cold Slaw.   Stewed Tomatoes.
Lemon pie.   Cheese.

THURSDAY.

Chicken Soup.
Celery.
Roast Beef, Horseradish.   Brown Potatoes.   String Beans.
Sliced Cucumbers.
Snow Pudding.   Coffee.

FRIDAY.

Mutton Broth.
Olives.
Roast Veal.   Mashed Potatoes.   Boiled Onions.
Chicken Salad.   Apple Pie.   Coffee.

SATURDAY.

Potato Soup.
Chicken Pie.   Asparagus.   Baked Apples.
Potatoes with Cream.   Lettuce.
Prune Pudding.   Coffee.

The Age of Elegance   115

MILK TOMATO SOUP

Put one quart of tomatoes over the fire and allow them to stew about ten minutes, add a pinch of soda, and when done foaming put them through a sieve. Heat one and one-half quarts of milk, to which has been added butter, pepper, and salt, and when boiling add the tomatoes, also hot, and remove from the fire immediately. Place in the tureen a few spoonfuls of rolled crackers (or bread cut in dice and well browned), pour the soup over this, and serve very hot.

CREAM POTATO SOUP

Pare and slice four large potatoes and cook with as little water as possible. When thoroughly done add one table-spoonful of butter, salt and pepper to taste, and mash very fine. Add one and one-half quarts of milk, and stir thoroughly, allow this to come slowly to a boil, turn into the soup tureen, add a small cup of whipped cream, and serve immeidately.

CREAM CHICKEN SOUP

Cut up chicken in cold water and simmer with very little salt; when cooked and cold take off grease. To one quart broth add one-half cup celery, boil in broth, season with white pepper. Rub to a smooth paste two tablespoons flour and two tablespoons butter, add to stock, and last one pint hot cream.

BOUILLON

Four pounds beef, two pounds bone, one tablespoon salt, four peppercorns, four cloves, two quarts cold water, one tablespoon mixed herbs; cut the meat and bone into small pieces, add the water, heat slowly, add the season-ing, simmer five hours. Boil down to three pints, strain, remove the fat, season with salt and pepper to taste, serve in cups. Boil one onion, half a carrot, and a turnip in it if you like.

EGG BALLS FOR SOUP

Boil four eggs twenty minutes, put in cold water, when cool cut carefully through the whites and remove yolks whole. They may be served in the soup whole or cut in quarters. Or put yolks in a bowl; rub to a paste; season with salt, pepper, and one teaspoon melted butter; moisten with yolk of one raw egg; shape it into balls about the size of a walnut; fry in butter. They can be boiled five minutes in the soup, but are better fried.

ROAST BEEF

The best pieces for roasting are the sirloin and rib pieces. When roasting in an oven, dash a cup of hot water over the meat; this checks the escape of the juice. Baste frequently with salt and water and the drippings. If your fire is hot, allow twelve minutes to the pound if you like the beef rare; more, if you prefer it well done. Thicken the gravy with browned flour.

BEEF A LA MODE

Take five or six pounds round of beef, rub with salt, and lard with salt pork. Put in a crock and cover with weak vinegar; into this cut one onion, one carrot, one turnip, a few whole peppers and cloves. Let this remain in vinegar several days. Take a porcelain kettle, put some beef drippings in when hot, put beef in, cover closely, let brown, then put in your spiced vinegar, cook three hours. When done take out and put one-half cup cream, one-fourth cup raisins, and one tablespoon sugar into gravy; thicken with browned flour; serve with potato dumplings.

PICKLE FOR BEEF OR PORK

Mix in four gallons water one and one-half pounds of sugar or molasses and two ounces saltpetre. If it is to last a month or two, put in six pounds salt. If you wish to keep it over summer put in nine pounds of salt. Boil all together gently, skim and let cool, put meat in vessel in which you wish to keep it, put the pickle on until it is covered and keep it for family use. Can be used after six weeks. After two months boil over, skim, and put in two ounces of sugar and one-half pound salt.

VEAL LOAF

Three pounds veal, three-quarters of a pound pork (fresh), chopped fine with the veal, butter the size of a large egg, melted, one teaspoonful onion juice, one teaspoonful grated nutmeg, one heaping tablespoonful capers, juice of one-half lemon, quarter of lemon rind grated, one teacupful grated bread crumbs, salt and pepper, red or black to taste, three eggs well beaten. Mix thoroughly and bake about three hours.

SMOTHERED CHICKEN (MOTHER'S WAY)

Clean chicken thoroughly, put it breast upward in a shallow pan, pour over it one cup boiling water, cover tightly to keep steam in, cook one-half hour. Then baste with the hot water, rub all over with melted butter, season with salt and pepper. Baste often, keep closely covered, cook till tender, and brown light brown. Thicken the gravy, add chopped parsley, salt, and pepper, and pour over chicken.

BAKED RED SNAPPERS

Take two pounds red snappers, remove bones, stuff with dressing as for chicken if you like, put in baking pan, dredge with flour, and sprinkle with pepper and salt. Take a couple strips bacon or salt pork, lay on dish, pour a little water in pan and bake about an hour, basting occasionally till done. Remove carefully to hot platter and pour over sauce made of drawn butter, with juice of lemon added. Very nice.

STUFFED POTATOES

Take large potatoes, bake until soft, and cut a round piece off the top of each. Scrape out the inside carefully, so as not to break the skin, mash the inside, working into it while hot, butter, salt, pepper, and about half a teaspoonful of cream for each potato and one well-beaten egg. Fill the skins with this mixture, and bake brown. Grated cheese or chopped cold meat of any kind can be added if liked.

POTATO PEARS

Mash and season half a dozen potatoes. Mold them while warm into the shape of small pears, dip them in the beaten yolk of egg, stick in the small end of each pear a clove (the large end of the clove in the potato) to represent the stem. Bake in a quick oven fifteen or twenty minutes till a rich brown. Success depends on thorough mashing and seasoning, and on baking long enough to heat them through.

TOMATO OYSTERS

Slice six good-sized tomatoes, cover with a quart of boiling water, add one even teaspoonful soda, boil fifteen minutes, add one pint of milk, and season as oysters.

CABBAGE COOKED WITH SOUR CREAM

Half-cup sour cream, half-cup vinegar, two or three teaspoons mustard, pepper black and red, salt. Put all together and let it almost boil, then put in half a cabbage chopped fine and let cook half an hour.

PEAS

Boil tender in salted water. Drain; add one cup of cream, a tablespoon butter, a little salt and pepper; thicken if liked.

DICE BEETS

Boil beets tender and cut in squares; put on vinegar diluted with water, a tablespoon butter, a little salt and pepper; and thicken with corn starch.

SPINACH

One peck spinach; boil twenty minutes in a quart of salted water, drain off the water and chop very fine. Take three tablespoonfuls of butter and small cup of stale bread crumbs and brown slightly in the butter, into which put the spinach and add an even tablespoonful of grated onion (if desired), and pepper and salt to taste. Garnish the dish with hard-boiled eggs.

FRIED PARSNIPS

Peel and boil parsnips; when done, drain, season with pepper and salt, dip first in melted butter, then in flour, and dust with sugar. Put two tablespoonfuls of drippings or lard into a frying pan; when hot put in enough parsnips to cover bottom of pan, fry brown on one side, then turn and brown on the other. Serve with roast pork.

CUCUMBER SALAD

Take cucumbers partially ripe, pare and slice very thin, place in weak salt and water for half an hour, then drain. Dressing for same: half-cup vinegar, half-cup sweet cream, two eggs, pepper and salt to taste, one teaspoonful flour, one teaspoonful sugar; let come to a boil, stirring constantly to keep from curdling (it is better cooked in a double boiler). Put cucumbers in till they become thoroughly heated; serve at once.

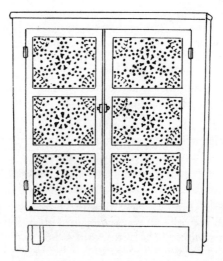

Nebraska Pioneer Cookbook

CHICKEN SALAD

Boil the fowls tender, and remove all the fat, gristle, and skin; mince the meat in small pieces, but do not hash it. To one chicken put twice and a half its weight in celery, cut in pieces of about one-quarter of an inch; mix thoroughly, and set it in a cool place,—the ice chest. In the meantime prepare a mayonnaise dressing, and when ready for the table pour this dressing over the chicken and celery, tossing and mixing it thoroughly. Set it in a cool place until ready to serve. Garnish with celery tips, or cold hard-boiled eggs, lettuce leaves from the heart, cold boiled beets, capers, or olives. Crisp cabbage is a good substitute for celery; when celery is not to be had, use celery vinegar in the dressing. Turkey also makes a fine salad.

SALMON SALAD

Take one can of salmon, add three cups of cabbage or celery chopped fine. Season one cup of vinegar with one-half tablespoon of salt, one of mustard, a little cayenne pepper, sugar, and a piece of butter the size of an egg. Let it boil, then stir in the yolks of four eggs. Pour this dressing over the salmon and cabbage, mix well and put in a dish, garnish with parsley and sliced lemon.

ENGLISH PLUM PUDDING

Soak one pound of stale bread in a pint of hot milk, and let it stand and cool. When cold, add to it one-half pound of sugar and the yolks of eight eggs beaten to a cream, one pound of raisins, stoned and floured, one pound of Zante currants, washed and floured, a quarter of a pound of citron, cut in slips and dredged with flour, one pound of beef suet, chopped finely and salted, one glass of wine, one glass of brandy, one nutmeg, ground, and a table-spoonful of mace, cinnamon, and cloves mixed; beat the whole well together, and, as the last thing, add the whites of the eight eggs, beaten to a stiff froth. Pour into a cloth, previously scalded and dredged with flour, tie the cloth firmly, leaving room for the pudding to swell, and boil six hours. Serve with wine or brandy sauce. It is best to prepare the ingredients the day before, and cover closely.

PRUNE PUDDING

Heat a little more than a pint of sweet milk to the boiling point, then stir in gradually a little cold milk in which you have rubbed smooth a heaping tablespoonful of corn starch. Add one-fourth cup of sugar or to suit your taste, three well-beaten eggs, about a teaspoonful of butter, and a little grated nutmeg. Let this come to a boil, then pour it in a buttered pudding-dish, first adding a cupful of stewed prunes, with the stones taken out. Bake from fifteen to twenty minutes, according to the state of the oven. Serve with or without sauce. A little cream improves it if poured over it when placed in saucers.

LEMON TART

Two cups sugar, one cup butter, six eggs, two lemons, two large tablespoonfuls brandy (if desired), one teaspoonful grated nutmeg. Beat butter and sugar together, add the whipped yolks, the juice of one lemon and the rind of two, the nutmeg, the brandy, and the stiffly beaten whites of the eggs. Bake in small pastry shells and use no top crust.

FRUIT CAKE

One pound butter, one pound sugar, one pound flour, twelve eggs beaten separately, four pounds raisins after they are stoned (chop in half), three pounds currants, two pounds citron, half pound almonds blanched and chopped, one pound figs chopped, one cup molasses, one teaspoonful soda stirred in it, one glass of any dark jelly, one large cup grated cocoanut, half pint brandy and sherry wine mixed, one tablespoonful cloves, two tablespoonfuls cinnamon, one teaspoonful nutmeg and ground mace mixed, one-fourth teaspoonful allspice. Mix sugar and butter to a cream first, add yolks beaten light, then jelly, molasses, brandy, and spices. Put all the fruit and nuts together, sprinkle a little flour (a large handful, not in the pound) over them, then add them a little at a time, alternating with the whites beaten very light and the flour until all is in. Beat five minutes and put in pan, bake slowly four hours.

Bills of Fare for One Week.

SUPPERS.

SUNDAY.

Cold Turkey.   Pickles.
Potato Salad.
Jam.   Sauce.   Cake.
Tea.

MONDAY.

Cold Meats.   Cream Potatoes.
Pickles.   Preserves.
Tea Biscuits.   Cake.   Sauce.
Tea.

TUESDAY.

Cold Boiled Ham.   Potato Cakes.
Toasted Cheese.   Pickles.
Parker House Rolls.   Peaches and Cream.
Chocolate.   Cake.

WEDNESDAY.

Cold Roast Mutton.   Saratoga Chips.
Sally Lunn.   Jelly.
Cake.   Sliced Pine Apple.
Tea.

THURSDAY.

Hash.   Poached Eggs.   Baked Potatoes.
Rolls.   Jam.
Cake and Sauce.
Cocoa.

FRIDAY.

Cold Roast Beef.   Potato Puffs.
Cream Sweet Breads.
Tea Biscuits.   Preserves.
Fresh Fruit.   Cake.
Tea.

SATURDAY.

Minced Veal with Poached Eggs.
Cream Biscuits.   Preserves.
Sauce and Cake.   Tea or Chocolate.

BEEF PATTIE

Three pounds beef chopped fine, three eggs well beaten, six crackers rolled fine, one tablespoon salt, one of melted butter, and one teaspoon of pepper, sage to taste; make into a loaf. Put a little water and a bit of butter in pan, baste often, bake an hour and a quarter. When cold slice thin.

CHICKEN HOLLANDAISE

Two coffee cups of the light and dark meat of the chicken chopped fine, one-half teacup of butter, two teacups boiling water, one teaspoon corn starch, yolks of two eggs, juice of half a lemon, one-half cup of celery chopped fine, one teaspoon chopped parsley, one teaspoon chopped onions. Mix butter and corn starch thoroughly together, melt in the chafing dish, add gradually the hot water and stir until it begins to thicken. Then add lemon juice, the beaten yolks, celery, onions, and parsley, pepper and salt to taste, stir well. In this sauce heat the chicken and serve immediately with buttered graham toast.

SCALLOPED FISH

Proportioned for six persons. One quart of boiled and flaked fish—white halibut or cod—put three tablespoonfuls of butter in a frying pan, and when melted add two tablespoonfuls of flour and stir until smooth and frothy. Gradually add one quart of milk and stir continually until it boils, then let it simmer for two minutes. Add two tablespoonfuls of Parmesan cheese, one teaspoonful of onion juice, one level teaspoon of salt, one-quarter teaspoon of pepper. Put juice of one-half of lemon in water in which the fish is boiled, do not boil too long or too fast or it will be hard and woolly. Sprinkle flaked fish with quarter teaspoonful of pepper and one level tablespoonful of salt. Put sauce in bottom of your dish (for individuals), then alternate until your dish is filled, finishing with sauce. Sprinkle with bread crumbs, and brown. This can be prepared in the morning and browned for supper; it does not hurt to stand.

POACHED EGGS

Serve poached eggs on slices of fried bread that are previously covered with the finest mince of hot (warmed-over) meat. Make the meat a mince of chicken or turkey, and add a few chopped truffles around the well-formed eggs and you have a dainty French dish.

WELSH RAREBIT

One-half pound cheese, two eggs, one tablespoon mustard, one-half teaspoon salt, one-half cup cream, pinch of cayenne pepper. Break cheese into small bits, put the ingredients in a pan over hot water, stir until cheese melts, spread over toast and serve.

CHEESE FONDA

Soak one cup dry bread crumbs in two scant cups rich milk, beat into this three eggs whipped very light, add one small teaspoon melted butter, one small teaspoon pepper, one small teaspoon salt, one-half pound of old cheese grated. Pour into a buttered baking dish, strew the top with dry bread crumbs, and bake a delicate brown in quick oven, serve immediately in the baking dish as it soon falls.

RUSSIAN SALAD

One quart cooked potatoes, cut in dice, one small onion chopped fine, one pint dark red pickled beets cut in dice, one cup of fresh apples cut in very small dice, one cup either chicken or veal cut fine, two herrings (soaked over night; remove bones, etc.), three hard-boiled eggs cut fine, small head celery, cut fine. For dressing, three eggs beaten well, add one tablespoonful French mustard, one teaspoonful each of salt and pepper, and two of salad oil, mix well and add one-half cup of best vinegar. The salad can be made without the beets and with plain vinegar.

EGG SALAD

For a family of twelve, fifteen eggs are required; boil hard and chop, then mix with salad dressing and sprinkle yolk of one egg over the top. Dressing proportions: one tablespoonful of vinegar to yolk of one egg, put vinegar on to boil, add the egg well beaten, season to taste with salt, pepper, butter, and mustard.

SARATOGA CHIPS

Peel good-sized potatoes, and slice them as evenly as possible. Drop them into ice water; have a kettle of very hot lard, as for cakes; put a few at a time into a towel and shake, to dry the moisture out of them, and then drop them into the boiling lard. Stir them occasionally, and when of a light brown take out with a skimmer, and they will be crisp and not greasy. Sprinkle salt over them while hot.

POTATO PUFFS

Two cups mashed potatoes, two tablespoons melted butter, beaten until creamy, then add two well-beaten eggs and one cup of cream, a little salt. Beat well, pour into a baking dish, spread butter over the top, and bake quickly a delicate brown.

SALLY LUNN

One pint potato sponge, one-half cup milk, one-fourth cup sugar, one teaspoonful salt, one large cooking-spoonful butter, yolks of two eggs. Mix butter and sugar together; add yolks, salt, and milk; mix well and add sponge with flour enough to make a stiff dough. If wanted for tea, set at 11 a.m., let rise until 1 o'clock, knead again, adding flour until it does not stick to the board, let rise until 4 o'clock. Roll out in two sheets, butter one and lay the other on top, cut out with biscuit cutter, let rise, and bake in a quick oven.

POTATO SPONGE

Three medium-sized potatoes, one-half pint Victor flour, one teaspoonful salt, one teaspoonful sugar, a pinch ginger and cinnamon. Boil potatoes in a pint of water; when done remove, mash very fine, and add the above ingredients. Mix thoroughly and scald with the potato water. When cool add one-half cake Fleischmann & Co.'s yeast dissolved in a little water. Thin with one pint cold water. Let rise over night. Keep in a cool place.

FRITTERS

One pint sweet milk, three eggs beaten separately, flour to make a thick batter. Beat milk and flour together; add the beaten yolks, a teaspoon of salt, and the stiffly beaten whites; sweeten lightly. Drop by spoonfuls into plenty of boiling lard, and fry until they puff way up. Eat hot with hard sauce—or they are good simply spread with butter and sugared.

SUNSHINE CAKE

Eleven whites of eggs, six yolks of eggs, one teaspoon cream of tartar, one and one-half cups sifted granulated sugar, one cup flour, one teaspoon extract of orange. Beat whites till stiff and flaky, then whisk in one-half the sugar, beat yolks very light and add flavor and one-half the sugar, put yolks and whites together and fold in flour and cream of tartar, mixing as quickly as possible. Bake fifty to sixty minutes in a slow oven, using angel cake pan.

JAM CAKE

One and one-half cups sugar, creamed with half cup of butter, whites of four eggs, cup of sweet milk, two and one-half cups of flour with two teaspoons of baking powder sifted into it. Beat till smooth and bake in two thick layers. Bake in a pretty quick oven, test with a wood toothpick, and take out the moment it is done. For the filling, get a twenty-five cent jar of the best red raspberry jam; it must be very thick or it will run. Use it all on the two layers, and pour a thin frosting over the top layer.

COCOANUT CAKE

One cup butter, two cups sugar, one-half cup milk, one-half cup water, three and one-half cups flour (measured after sifting), two teaspoons baking powder, whites of eight eggs (if eggs are small use ten); bake in layers.

Filling: Two cups sugar, less than one-half cup water (enough to dissolve the sugar); let it cook until it strings. Have beaten up the whites of two eggs (not stiff), pour the boiling syrup over this, beating all the time, flavor with lemon or orange. Put the layers together with the icing, sprinkling grated cocoanut over each; finish the cake with icing and grated cocoanut. One cocoanut is sufficient for a large cake.

BROWN STONE FRONT CAKE

One and one-half cups sugar, one-half cup butter (cream sugar and butter), two eggs beaten separately, one-half teaspoonful soda, one teaspoonful baking powder, one cup sour cream, two squares of chocolate soaked in one cup of boiling water, three scant cups of flour. Mix and bake as any cake.

Caramel Filling: One cup of cream, one and one-half cups sugar. Boil ten minutes or until almost stringy. Remove from stove and beat until very stiff. If too stiff add a little cold cream. Flavor with vanilla.

HERMITS

One cup of brown sugar, half cup of molasses, half cup of butter, one cup of chopped raisins, three eggs, one teaspoon cloves, cinnamon, allspice, ginger, two teaspoons of soda. Beat sugar and butter together, then add molasses after being beaten to a foam with soda, then spices, eggs, and lastly raisins, and flour enough to roll. Cut out and bake in moderate oven twelve to fifteen minutes.

SAND TARTS

Two cups sugar, one cup butter, two eggs, flavor to the taste, flour enough to roll. Cut out and take one egg well beaten to wet top of tarts and sprinkle with sugar before putting in the oven. Bake in a moderately hot oven until lightly browned, about ten minutes.

REFRESHING DRINKS FOR SUMMER

Put into a tumbler about two tablespoonfuls of broken ice, two tablespoonfuls of chocolate syrup, three table-spoonfuls of whipped cream, one gill of milk, and a half a gill of soda-water, from a siphon bottle, or Apollinaris water. Stir well before drinking. A tablespoonful of va-nilla ice-cream is a desirable addition. It is a delicious drink, even if the soda or Apollinaris water and ice-cream be omitted. A plainer drink is made by combining the syrup, a gill and a half of milk, and the ice, and shaking well.

RASPBERRY SHRUB

Four quarts of red raspberries to one of vinegar; let stand four days, then strain. To each pint of juice add a pound of sugar. Boil twenty minutes. Bottle and keep in a dry, cool place.

GRAPE WINE

One quart of grape pulp, skins and seeds, one cup of white sugar. Put in jar and let stand until fermented, strain it, return to jar, and let stand for a week or two. Draw off the wine, bottle, and seal.

STRAWBERRY WINE

To the juice of three quarts of strawberries, mashed and strained, add one-half the quantity of red currant juice. Put to each quart of fruit juice one quart of water and one pound of loaf sugar. Ferment it in a clean, sweet cask, leaving the bung out. When fermentation has finished, put into bottles and cork it for use. It is a very pleasant wine for invalids and also for cooking purposes.

The Age of Elegance   129

CREAM CANDY

To the unbeaten white of an egg, add a tablespoon of water; mix in one pound of confectioners' sugar and flavoring to suit the taste. Work well and mold into fancy shapes, using cocoanut, chocolate, nuts, figs, dates, etc., as trimmings.

MARSH MALLOWS

Dissolve one-half pound of gum arabic in one pint of water, strain and add one-half pound of fine sugar and place over the fire, stirring constantly until the syrup is dissolved and consistency of honey. Add gradually the whites of four eggs, well beaten, stir the mixture until it becomes somewhat thin and does not adhere to the finger, flavor to taste and pour into a tin slightly dusted with powdered starch. When cool divide into small squares.

CHOCOLATE CARAMELS

Three pounds brown sugar, one cup milk, three-fourths cup butter, one-half pound Walter Baker & Co.'s chocolate. Cook until a drop of mixture forms a firm ball in cold water. Stir all the time towards the last. Pour into a buttered pan and cut into squares when cold.

MOLASSES CANDY

Two cups of molasses, one cup of sugar, tablespoonful of vinegar, small lump of butter. Boil rapidly until it drops brittle into cold water, pour into buttered tins, and when cold pull till it is white.

Kate McPhelim Cleary, who lived in Nebraska from 1884 to 1898 and wrote poems, stories, and sketches of local life for the literary journals of the time, also turned out an occasional piece on cookery for women's magazines. In "The Storeroom: Its Convenience and Contents," she describes the stocking of a well-supplied pantry in the genteel turn-of-the-century household:

Putting aside jams, jellies, and home-made conserves, of which I shall assume you have a varied supply, I will merely mention a few other articles which you will find it wise to have in reserve. First of all, a thick ham and a flitch of breakfast bacon. The possibilities of both are too well known to need particular mention. Next, a couple of dried tongues. These, after being cured . . . may be dried by hanging in a moderately warm place for about three weeks. At the end of that time they will resemble dark wood to the sight and touch. They will keep indefinitely, and if soaked over night before cooking will be found tender and of peculiarly delicious flavor.

Then if you do not use olive oil, or even if you do, and are too hurried to make a mayonnaise at times, by all means keep on hand a Mason jar filled with cooked salad dressing; not the boughten salad dressing, which is expensive and of which one quickly tires, but the home-made kind that is equally good, and that will keep for months in the hottest weather without moulding or souring, no matter how frequently opened. Here is a reliable recipe: Yolks of six eggs, two level teaspoonfuls of white pepper, three level teaspoonfuls of salt, six level teaspoonfuls of white sugar, six level teaspoonfuls of mustard, two table-spoonfuls of melted butter, and twelve tablespoonfuls of vinegar. Beat the eggs thoroughly. Mix the spices well while dry, then add the vinegar, stirring all till smooth. Now add the beaten eggs and melted butter and cook all in custard kettle, stirring till thick and smooth. Put into a glass jar and keep in a cool place. When required for use take a couple of tablespoonfuls—it should be very thick but not stiff—and dilute to the consistency desired with sweet cream, and, if the salad is to be a trifle sharp, the juice of half a lemon or a dash of vinegar.

Nothing is more satisfactory to "fall back upon" than deviled crabs. In purchasing the cans of crab meat be careful not to buy that which is already seasoned, and which is inferior to the plain crab meat prepared at home. . . . To a one-pound can of crab meat add the pungent, yellowish dressing [directions for which are given above] to taste—about two tablespoonfuls will be sufficient. Add a good shake of celery salt, a dessertspoonful of minced onion, one tablespoonful of finely shredded parsley, one hard-boiled egg chopped fine, and one raw egg beaten very light. Have the crab shells buttered and laid in a dripping pan. Fill these with the mixture, which must be stiff rather than "runny." Sprinkle over each some dry, sifted bread or cracker crumbs. Pour evenly on top of each a tablespoonful of melted

The Age of Elegance   131

butter. Set the pan containing the shells in a moderately hot oven and bake for about twenty minutes, or until the deviled crabs are a golden brown. Remove and serve in the shells, red hot. This is not expensive, is far more easily prepared than it sounds, and makes a most acceptable dish. As an entrée, or for a late supper it is particularly acceptable.

Of course there will be kept in the storeroom canned tomatoes from which, when hurried, to quickly evolve a soup, a sauce, or add the touch of distinction to a stew. Even if it is found cheaper and more convenient to buy the tomatoes canned, as under some conditions it certainly is, by all means put up some at home for the sake of having what cannot be purchased—pure tomato juice. Having a bushel of sound, ripe tomatoes, scald and skin them. Put them in a granite or porcelain-lined kettle. Boil till they are well broken, but not mushy. Then, having the jars prepared as for ordinary canning, lift with a skimmer all the thick part of the tomato into the jars. This will come in handy for vegetable soups and thick Creole stews. Strain the remainder through a wire strainer, return to the fire, add salt and red pepper to taste, and, when boiling hot, pour into bottles and seal at once. By the way, do not—as do most young housekeepers, and some old ones, too—attempt to seal the bottles by pouring melted wax over the corks. Have the wax hot in an old tin cup, and in it dip the corks of the bottles; reverse at once and there results a fine, smooth cap for the corks. . . .

Keep in the storeroom, too, a few cans of peas and mushrooms. The former should be the best—the French peas, as, unless for soup, no other kind are really satisfactory. But the cheaper grades of mushrooms, which may be procured from fifteen to twenty cents a can, are quite good enough for mushroom sauce, quail pie, and even for chicken patties. . . .

There will undoubtedly be mince-meat on the shelves, if it be winter. In summer a similar compound and delectable substitute, Banbury mixture, is recommended. For this, which will keep a year at least, and may be served in shells, rissoles, or vol-au-vents of puff paste, here is Catherine Owen's reliable rule: Half a pound of currants, half a pound of strained honey, four ounces of candied citron, four ounces of candied lemon peel —both cut fine; one teaspoonful of cinnamon, half a teaspoonful of cloves, half a teaspoonful of allspice—all ground. Also the grated rind of an orange, and a large wineglassful of brandy. Mix well. . . .

A few cans of shrimps which, with the dressing mentioned,

can be speedily converted into salad, a bottle of Worcestershire sauce, a few ounces of bay leaves, so desirable for some soups; a bottle of olives for garnishing, a small bottle of curry powder, an Edam or pineapple cheese, a bottle of good claret with which to make a frappe or a fruit salad, half a dozen boxes of gelatine,—with these one will be proof against the panic which unexpected visitors, however welcome they may be, sometimes occasion in well-regulated households. . . .

The late Victorian period was rightfully noted for its elegant dining: business and professional men organized discussion clubs distinguished more by their gastronomical than their intellectual merit, and their wives prided themselves on being able to bring off seven-course dinner parties with complete aplomb. In presentations on quail ("for women of intelligence, culture and limited knowledge of this particular branch of the culinary art") and bananas ("it is astonishing that a fruit so delicious, so cheap, and so procurable at all seasons as are bananas, should be seldom served in novel and attractive desserts"), Mrs. Cleary offers recipes that illustrate the elaborate cuisine of the era.

ROAST QUAIL

"Baked" is perhaps the more explicit word to use. Unless in the houses of the very wealthy, where spits and open fireplaces are provided for the purpose, roasting, in the correct sense of the word, is neither understood nor practiced in this country. Truss, if you desire to serve your quail in English fashion, by bringing the head around, and tucking it under the wing. Skewer the legs so that they shall stand erect. Rub each with a generous pinch of white pepper, one-fourth of a teaspoonful of salt, one teaspoonful of lemon juice, and one teaspoonful of melted butter. Daub the breasts well with butter. Place in dripping pan a layer of very thin slices of fat ham or bacon. Set the quail on these. When done, which should be in fifteen minutes in a brisk oven, remove skewers and place pan on the oven grate to allow the birds to brown. Serve on a platter surrounded by a hedge of water cress, outside of which you have arranged an overlapping row of croutons.

CROUTONS

Croutons are cut from stale bread. You may make diamonds of them, or shape them in any other fanciful manner. Fry them in deep fat, which has been brought to the same degree of heat requisite for fritters. When a golden brown, remove with a perforated skimmer. Drain on soft paper—newspaper will do—and serve while hot.

SALMI OF QUAIL

If judiciously made, this dish is very acceptable to those who approve meat served in savory and piquant sauces. Fresh quail, half cooked for the purpose, is used by those who do not consider cost. From the remains of roast, broiled, or even fried quail, an epicurean dish can, however, be served. Carve your birds in neat pieces. Set aside. Take the skin, gristle and any bones you may have. Hack half a pound of the round of beef into dice. Put all together in a saucepan. Sprinkle over half a small carrot (cut up), two sprigs of shredded parsley, one small sliced onion, three or four leaves of celery, half a bay leaf, a pinch of thyme and tablespoonful of butter. Fry all together till the spoon you stir with is covered with a glaze, then add half a pint of stock. If you have not this, water must answer. Simmer all slowly and steadily for an hour. Strain your broth. Blend a tablespoonful of flour with a little white wine. Pour into the broth, and stir till smooth and bub-

bling. Put in your cold quail and let simmer for five minutes. Season to taste with salt and pepper. Dish. Pour the
sauce over. Garnish with crisp, white celery tops and
slices of bitter orange.

QUAIL PIE

Chop fine one pound of round steak. Take the inferior
parts of your birds. Put all together in a saucepan with a
medium-sized sliced onion, half a small carrot (sliced),
one bay leaf and half a stalk of celery. Cover all with soft
cold water. Let this cook in a custard kettle for two hours.
Joint your quail, fry quickly for about five minutes in two
tablespoonfuls of butter, and remove. Put in the bottom of
a deep baking dish a thin layer of cold boiled ham. On this
place a layer of the quail. Cover the quail with slices of
hard-boiled eggs, cut lengthwise, in quarters, then scatter
in a few shreds of the ham. Over this throw finely-cut
fresh parsley. Then repeat all till the dish is filled. Here
and there in the cavities insert button mushrooms, balls of
forcemeat and halved slices of lemon. Drain your broth.
Add to it flour smoothly blended with a little cold water.
To a quart of liquid allow a heaping tablespoonful of
flour. Add pepper and salt to taste, also one teaspoonful of
Worcestershire sauce. Pour all into your arranged dish,
and set aside while you make a rich puff paste. Or if you
have had sufficient forethought to make your puff paste
some hours ahead, and set it on the ice till required, so
much the better. Cover the dish. Make a fancy knot of the
paste on top. Glaze with half-beaten white of egg, and
bake in a moderate oven for an hour and a quarter. It is
well to cover the top with cardboard for the first twenty
minutes.

QUAIL WITH MUSHROOMS

Prepare and cook as directed for roast quail. Reduce by
rapid boiling, one pint of bouillon to two-thirds of a pint.
Brown in a separate saucepan, one tablespoonful of butter, adding to it one tablespoonful of flour. Stir till bub-
bling, then strain in your beef broth. Stir steadily till
smooth. Add a can of mushrooms. Season to taste with
pepper, salt and celery salt. Remove quail to hot platter.
Pour the mushroom sauce around, not over the birds.

Garnish with lemon and parsley, and serve at once. If the sauce be still too pale of tint, add a couple of drops of caramel.

QUAIL IN MAYONNAISE

Heap neatly-trimmed pieces of cold cooked quail on a bed of crisp and curly lettuce leaves. Pour over the mound a mayonnaise dressing. Around the edge lay loosely a few sprays of parsley. Garnish with beet root cut in fanciful shapes, yolks of hard-boiled eggs, and stoned olives.

BANANA ROLY-POLY

Make a rich puff paste or a short biscuit crust, as preferred. Roll this into a large, thin square. Trim off the edges with a sharp knife. Peel the bananas—three will prove sufficient for a roly-poly of ordinary size—and slice them on half of the pastry. Sprinkle with sugar, and fold over the other half of the pastry till the points lie together, and the roly-poly is the shape of a halved diamond. Of course the crust may be rolled in the long, old-fashioned bolster if desired, but if simply folded in the style suggested the pastry is lighter, the appearance is prettier, and there are no half-soggy inner folds to be eschewed. With a stiff feather, or with the fingers if they are "fairy light," gloss the top over with the half-beaten white of an egg, and shower this as evenly as possible with granulated sugar. A little way in from the edge press the crust together with the back of a knife, in order to retain the juice, but do not pinch the edges. Remove as carefully as possible to a baking sheet. Use a pancake turner to assist in doing this deftly. Bake from twenty to thirty minutes in a hot oven. Serve at once with a sauce made as follows: Pare thinly the rind of two lemons. Place these, with one cup of cold water, in the upper part of a custard kettle. Set this on the stove and simmer for ten minutes. Then remove the rind, add the strained juice of the lemons and one and a half cupfuls of sugar. Boil this hard for five minutes, then set the upper part of the custard kettle into the lower, wherein the water is boiling, and into the sirup stir the well-beaten yolks of two eggs. Stir steadily till the mixture is smooth, then beat vigorously with an egg-beater for about three minutes, and serve.

BANANA TRIFLE

Line a dessert dish with macaroons, lady's-fingers, or any other light cake which has been dipped in sherry, catawba, or strong lemonade; set this aside, then whip solid one pint of ice-cold cream which has been twenty-four hours rising. Then add, mixing in lightly, half a cupful of powdered sugar and a teaspoonful of any preferred extract. Peel and slice into this three large bananas, heap all in the center of the prepared dish, and dot the white mound over with fresh strawberries or raspberries, or both. If the latter are not procurable, use instead blanched almonds, candied cherries, and thin strips of angelica. Keep the trifle on ice if it must wait, but if possible serve soon after it is ready. This is a delicious as well as a beautiful dessert for a summer supper.

BANANA CREAM WITH JELLY

This dish, which the writer ventures to assert is strictly original, is rather elaborate and somewhat troublesome to prepare, but it is so sightly and so delicious that it forms a *pièce de résistance* for the supper table, compared to which the ordinary moulded jellies seem commonplace. Divide in equal parts the contents of one box of gelatine. On each portion pour a teacupful of cold water. In an hour's time pour upon one portion of the gelatine a teacupful of boiling water. Add a teacupful and a quarter of sugar, the grated rind and juice of two lemons, and a teacupful of pale sherry or catawba. A dark wine will not answer. In place of wine, take a teacupful of the sirup poured from canned pineapples. If this is not at hand, add to another half-teacupful of boiling water the juice and grated rind of an extra lemon, and the same of a large orange. Now stir all well and strain through a flannel bag or an old napkin, the center of which has been wrung out of hot water. This liquid is to be divided into two equal parts. It will be of a pale amber tint. If a shade deeper in tint is wanted and the yellow paste used by confectioners for that purpose is not to be had, grate the rind of another orange, steep it for a few minutes in barely enough alcohol to cover it, and strain through a bit of muslin into one-half the jelly. Pour this into a mould which has been rinsed with cold water, but not dried, and set in a cool place. Then color the other half of the jelly a pale green with extract of spinach, or a tiny speck of the regular leaf coloring which professionals use, add a few drops of Pistachio flavoring, and set where it will not harden. When the first layer of jelly is almost firm, give attention to the half box of gelatine which has not hitherto been touched beyond adding to it a cupful of cold water. Pour upon it now one and a half teacupfuls of boiling water, the grated rind and juice of two lemons, and two-thirds of a teacupful of granulated sugar. Stir well, and strain, as for jelly. Then force into it, through a press or ordinary colander, two large or three small bananas. Stir, and set in a cool place. When this latter is partially congealed, whip slightly one pint of thick, sweet cream. Beat into the cream the flavored gelatine, containing the mashed banana, one tablespoonful at a time. Now beat hard with the most efficacious utensil possessed, be it an egg-beater or merely a slit spoon. Were the cream beaten solid *at first*, the additional whipping required to incorporate the banana, would cause the compound—which should be smooth as blanc-mange—to become buttery. When all ingredients have been reduced to a smooth and snowy mass, take the mould in which the yellow jelly is now firm, pour in the banana cream and set this away to harden. When this is firm, pour upon it the green jelly which has been kept in a liquid state, although not at all hot. Set on ice till ready to serve, then dip the mould for an instant in hot water, gently loosen the jelly at the edges with the finger tips, cover with a dessert dish, quickly reverse, and remove the mould. The movement will reveal a mound or brick, the base of which is clear, green, transparent jelly, the center of opaque cream, and the top a crown of light gold. This must be used while fresh. Of course the jellies may be reversed, having the green on the top, etc. Or if there be not time or inclination for all this labor, the banana cream alone may be made, moulded and served.

If the proportions of nineteenth-century recipes seem large and the menus rich and heavy—well, they were. Plumpness was a sign of health; one ate to "keep his strength up." In the

Nebraska Pioneer Cookbook

summer of 1894, Willa Cather, then a university student and the Lincoln *Journal*'s literary and drama critic, wrote a series of stories on a Chautauqua at Crete for the Lincoln *Evening News*. The Chautauqua—a combination Sunday school, fine arts institute, and week-long picnic—was a popular form of entertainment and attracted a considerable amount of attention locally. In a facetious description of the Chautauqua dining hall, a rival journalist poked light-hearted fun at the hearty appetite of one young woman, most likely Willa:

> Loud young lady at first table on right; one of a circle of gig-gling girls and tender youths, outer edge of Lincoln's four hundred. Very pretty, very self-conscious and significantly aggressive. Profusely decorated straw-hat; pointed russet shoes. Diet liberal and rapidly swallowed to gain time for trivial conversation. Turned up her nose at me and looked exasperatingly saucy. . . .
>
> As regards quantity of nourishment disposed of, it is but scant justice to place my companion at the head of the list. This is her inventory: Three potatoes (extra size); two pieces of ham with wide fringes of fat, two by four; two ditto of a strongly and powerful spiced sausage, eight inches in diameter; six hot biscuits; one third of all the butter there was on the table; a modicum of Boston beans; one glass of milk; two pickles (assorted); three schooners of ice tea with extra ice thrown in and two pieces of chocolate cake thickly cut. There was a wind up of salted almonds, which I had been considerate enough to provide.
>
> This is what she called—not without a little hysterical laugh—a light supper. And still the ladies of the W.C.A. do not entirely despair of realizing a profit from the dining hall.

On July 10, 1896, William Jennings Bryan, a young Nebraska lawyer, won the Democratic presidential nomination and launched a national political career with his famous "Cross of Gold" speech. An ardent prohibitionist in later years, he drew huge crowds on the Chautauqua circuit as well as the campaign trail with his fiery oratory. He also had a notorious capacity for food. "The man expended a terrific amount of energy in each of his orations, as is evidenced by the fabulous quantities of food he consumed on an active campaign without suffering any appreciable impairment of his health," writes political commen-

tator Gerald W. Johnson. "A man who ate like Bryan had to expend energy at a furious rate; had he not done so, he would either have blown out every gasket in his internal mechanism, or he would have ended the tour weighing seven hundred pounds." Shortly after Bryan's selection to oppose William McKinley in the 1896 race, which centered on the question of the gold standard versus the free coinage of silver, this tongue-in-cheek story appeared in the Omaha *World-Herald* under the head "Drinks of the Campaign":

NEW YORK, July 25. "McKinley's Delight," the "Free Silver Fizz," the "Gold Cocktail" and others of their kind have already appeared in the up-to-date cafes, a fact which argues well for the exuberance with which the presidential campaign will be pushed from now on.

It is a painful fact for all right-minded bartenders to contemplate that both of the presidential candidates are abstainers. McKinley drinks nothing stronger than seltzer, while Bryan draws the line on the other side of ginger ale and sarsaparilla. The knights of the bar are, however, finding solace in the fact that

Nebraska Pioneer Cookbook

their old-time enemy, the prohibitionists, will be sadly discomfited by having to face two men with such anti-Kentuckian proclivities.

The morning after the announcement of McKinley's nomination, "McKinley's Delight" dawned upon the world, and on the same day that Bryan secured the plum at Chicago the "Free Silver Fizz" was born. Neither of these drinks is a temperance affair by any means. A man who knows whereof he speaks says that four of "McKinley's Delights" will render anyone blind, mentally and physically, while six "Free Silver Fizzes" have been known to cause immense damage, including the following:

One free fight; escape in hansom cab to avoid arrest; kicking the windows out of the said cab later; awful clubbing from the policeman called by cabby to arrest kicker; one night in station house, sharing same cell with habitual bum; one $20 fine in court next morning and a promise to pay cabby $33 for injuries to cab; subsequent bill from doctor for dressing wounds caused by policeman's club; one new suit of clothes to replace that ruined in two fights; one terrible family row caused by bogus explanation of absence from home; several terrible shocks to self-esteem caused by reading in newspapers full accounts of disgraceful happenings; unkind jokes by friends; chilly greetings by women friends of wife; one call from minister and long lecture on folly of intemperance; one cyclone battle with mother-in-law, to say nothing of ruffled feelings, loss of self-respect, bodily pains from policeman's clubs, monetary loss and mental suffering equal in all to $1,000.

Six drinks of a drink that can do all this shows that the "Free Silver Fizz" is something very much out of the ordinary. Here is the way the man who invented the drink mixes it:

A long, thin glass is set out, with two or three small lumps of crystal ice. Then the barkeeper, making an ostentatious pretense of washing and drying his hands, produces a large, fat, juicy lime. This he cuts in half. A silver strainer is laid over the glass lip. With his fingers the juice of the lime is squeezed onto the strainer and allowed to percolate through the holes and on to the ice.

Then an ordinary thin drinking glass and a bottle of gin are set before the interested and thirsting customer. It is the etiquet of the fashionable bar that in the concoction of the "fizz" the patron shall be the judge of the amount of spirits that he at the moment requires.

The modicum of gin is poured in upon the ice and lime juice, and then the bartender interrogates, "Vichy, seltzer or carbonated water?" The selection is made and the effervescent water is squirted into the glass, being deftly stirred in the meanwhile with a silver spoon. It must be drunk while "hot," that is, while foaming.

One patron who ordered a "Free Silver Fizz," merely to show his political learning, took two sips from the glass, and then placing it on the bar, said to the bartender, calmly, but plainly: "You're a fake."

The bartender took the insult blandly and the man with the glass took another sip, and again placing it upon the bar said:

"You're a fake. That's just an ordinary every day gin rickey. I have been drinking four of these every twenty-four hours for the past six months, and I repeat, you're a fake."

"Hush! Not so loud. You're right. I'm a fake. But the drink's all right, ain't it? We've got to change the names of the drinks every few months; that's the reason I've got to stand here quiet and peaceful with my hands at my side, listening to you call me a fake. That's a gin rickey, sure enough, but from now on until November, it's a 'Free Silver Fizz.' What it will be next year heaven only knows. You know a thing or two. Here's another new one, 'McKinley's Delight.' This is on me if you recognize it. If you don't, you pay."

This was agreed to and in a couple of minutes the new drink was on the bar. The knowing one took a couple of sips, looked meditatively at the ceiling, took another sip and looked thoughtfully upon the floor, again he swallowed some of the mixture, with a reminiscent glance at the glass.

"You would catch a novice with that, but I'm too old a hand. That's a gin crusta and it's more deadly than the rickey or silver fizz, as you call it."

"You don't pay; you're right," said the barkeeper.

This is the way to fashion a "McKinley's Delight": Fill a mixing glass half full of fine ice, add three dashes of gum syrup, two dashes of Maraschino, the juice of a quarter of lemon, two dashes Payschaud or Angostura bitters and one jigger of gin; mix, peel the rind from a large lemon and fit rind into the bottom of glass, moisten edge of the glass with a piece of lemon and dip it into the sugar, which gives it a frosty look, strain the mixture into thin prepared glass; trim with fruit and serve.

All the fashionable drinks now have as a basis gin—Holland, Plymouth or Old Tom, the kind our great grandfathers used to drink providing they were not temperance folks. There is one new drink just brought to New York from the south which, however, has no gin in it. It is called a "white plush," and is simply made. Into a long, slender glass is poured four fingers of whisky and then the glass is filled to the brim with ice cold milk. It's a stiff drink for a novice, but the old campaigner will tell you that you can drink it all day long without being hurt.

The iceberg is a new name, but the drink is old. It is made in a large glass half filled with cracked ice. A good dose of creme de menthe is thrown in and then the glass is filled with seltzer or Vichy. It is a cooling drink and not too powerful.

The best of them are, however, the old standbys, champagne cup, claret cup and champagne punch. Here is the newest way to make them:

Champagne Cup—Squeeze the juice of one lemon in a pitcher that will hold five pints. Sweeten with one tablespoonful of sugar, then add two ponies of red curaçao, one bottle of plain soda and two slices of cucumber rind. Pour in three pints of champagne, adding about a quarter of a pound of cracked ice. Then mix thoroughly with a spoon and ornament the punch with a few strawberries, some thin slices of pineapple, finely sliced orange and a half bunch of fresh mint. Send it to the table with champagne glasses.

Claret Cup—Have a glass pitcher that will hold two and one-half quarts. Squeeze in the juice of three lemons, add four table-spoonfuls of powdered sugar, two ponies of red curaçao and two slices of cucumber rind, then pour in three pints of claret and a pint of elysmie or apollinaris. Mix thoroughly and add a good sized piece of ice. Decorate with small pieces of orange, berries of any kind and some fresh mint. Serve in punch glasses.

Champagne Punch—Have a punch bowl large enough to hold three quarts. Prepare a pot of oolong tea and set aside to cool. Pour one pony of arrack into the bowl, two wine glasses of Rhine wine, one pony of brandy, one pony of Maraschino, one bottle of plain soda and one quart of champagne, then strain in the prepared tea. Mix thoroughly together with a ladle; then put in about a pound of ice. Peel a medium sized banana, slice thin and scatter over the punch, slice an orange and add.

Miscellaneous Recipes

N O NINETEENTH-CENTURY cookbook or women's magazine
was complete without a section of "miscellaneous receipts" designed to qualify the housewife as her own laun-
derer, dry cleaner, window washer, pest exterminator, cos-
metician, and general handyman. And in an age—by a contemporary physician's account—"when sulphur and molasses was
given as a blood purifier; when asafoetida was placed in a little
bag and hung around the neck to prevent contagious diseases;
when bacon rind or bread-and-milk poultice or possibly fresh
warm cow manure as a poultice was used to 'ripen' boils; when
a red flannel or kerosene-soaked rag or fried onions was
swathed around the throat for sore throat; when onion syrup
was made for a cough," the homemaker needed a repertory of
cures for everything from corns to catarrh.

Kitchen Helps

BREAD CRUMBS

All scraps of bread should be dried and rolled very fine
to use instead of cracker crumbs for cutlets and other
meats.

COOKING BUTTER

One pound kidney suet cut in small pieces and melted over a slow fire; add one pound butter, melt, and strain through a sieve.

VANILLA EXTRACT

To one vanilla bean cut in small pieces, add half a pint of alcohol and let stand for several weeks before using.

LEMON EXTRACT

Pare a lemon, being careful to use only the outside yellow, put in a jar and cover with alcohol, and let stand for several weeks before using.

BAKING POWDER

One pound pure cream of tartar, half pound common baking soda, quarter of a pound corn starch; sift six or seven times together, put away in an air-tight jar; ready for use at once.

Household Hints

SOAP

Five pounds lard or five and one-half pounds cracklings, one can of lye, one and one-half gallons water. Stir occasionally the first day, then set for three days. Cook until clear. Let set until hard and cut into bars.

WASHING FLUID

One can Babbit's lye dissolved in one gallon rain water; let cool, and add 10 cents' worth of salts of tartar and 10 cents' worth of ammonia. Use in washing and boiling water, a half teacupful to one-half boiler of water.

Miscellaneous Recipes

SOLUTION FOR TAKING OUT STAINS

Half pound chloride of lime, one and a half pounds sal soda; put both in a jar and pour one gallon of boiling water over, stir until dissolved, then strain and bottle. Wet the stain with the solution and lay in sun.

HINTS ON WASHING

Clothes should not be soaked over night; it gives them a grey look, and the soiled parts lying against the clean portions streak them. Rub the clothes in warm—not hot—water, for hot water sets, in place of removing the dirt. Wash flannels in luke-warm water, and avoid rubbing soap upon flannels.

TO KEEP BLUE CALICOES BRIGHT AND FRESH

The first time they are washed, put them in water with a cupful of spirits of turpentine to each pail of water. This will set the color, and they will always look well.

CLEANING SILKS

To renovate silk, rip and dust the garment; lay the pieces on an old sheet; take half a cup of ox-gall, half a cup of ammonia, and half a pint of tepid soft water; mix; sponge the silk on both sides, especially the soiled places; then roll on a round stick (old broom handle), being careful about wrinkles. Silk thus cleaned and dried needs no ironing, and keeps the lustre. Try woolens the same way.

TO CLEAN CORSETS

Take out the steels at front and sides, then scrub thoroughly with tepid or cold lather of white Castile soap, using a very small scrubbing brush. Do not lay them in water. When quite clean, let cold water run on them freely from the spigot to rinse out the soap thoroughly. Dry, without ironing (after pulling lengthwise until they are straight and shapely), in a cool place.

CLEANING KID GLOVES

The simplest and most successful method of cleaning kid gloves is to buy a pint of naphtha, price 10 cents, of any dealer in burning fluids; wash your kid gloves in it as if it were water, rubbing the parts soiled most. Wash two or three times in clean fluid, according to the needs of the soiled gloves. The usual care should be taken, as this fluid is highly explosive, much the same as kerosene.

SHOE POLISH

To restore the color of black kid boots, take a small quantity of black ink, mix it with the white of an egg, and apply with a soft sponge.

TO CLEAN SILVER

Table silver should be cleaned at least once or twice a week, and can easily be kept in good order and polished brightly in this way: Have your dish pan half full of boiling water; place your silver in so that it may become warm; then with a soft cloth dipped into the hot water, soaped and sprinkled with powdered borax, scour the silver well; then rinse in clean hot water; dry with a clean, dry cloth.

TO WHITEN KNIFE HANDLES

The ivory handles of knives sometimes become yellow from being allowed to remain in dish water. Rub them with sandpaper till white. If the blades have become rusty from careless usage, rub them also with sandpaper, and they will look as nice as new.

TO WASH WINDOWS

Have a pail partly filled with tepid water, throw in a teaspoonful of powdered borax, have one small chamois dipped into the borax water to wash the windows, then with a dry chamois rub the window dry and polish. In this way windows may be cleaned in a very few moments, and not wet the carpets or tire the person.

FURNITURE POLISH

One tablespoonful sweet oil; one tablespoonful lemon juice; one tablespoonful corn starch.

MOTHS IN CARPETS

A good way to kill them is to take a coarse towel and wring it out of clean water. Spread it smoothly on the carpet, then iron it dry with a good hot iron, repeating the operation on all suspected places, and those least used. It does not injure the carpet in the least. It is not necessary to press hard, heat and steam being the agents, and they do the work effectually on worms and eggs.

BEDBUGS

Close the outside doors and windows and burn brimstone, and you will not have any trouble with bedbugs, as we know from experience. Twelve years ago I bought a farm I now own, and the house was alive with them. I heated an iron red hot, placed it in a large kettle, placing brimstone on it, and left it twenty-four hours. Have not seen a bug since.

CURES FOR HOUSEHOLD PESTS

Rats are said to have such a dislike for potash, that if it is powdered and scattered around their haunts, they will leave them. A piece of rag well soaked in a solution of cayenne is a capital thing to put into rat and mice holes, as they will not attempt to eat it. A plug of wood, covered with a piece of flannel so prepared, may be used to fill up the holes. Cockroaches and ants have a similar dislike of cayenne, and a little strewed about a cellar will keep it clear of them.

PASTE FOR SCRAP-BOOKS

On wash days there is always enough thick starch left, or sticking to the sides of the pan, to last through the week for paste. If wanted in large quantities, of course, starch would be expensive, but scrap-books can be made merely by saving what would otherwise have been thrown away. It makes a very nice, smooth paste, and a little of it goes a great way. It will keep a week in a cool place, even in summer.

Hygienic Recipes

HAIR INVIGORATOR

Bay rum, one pint; alcohol, one-half pint; castor oil, one-half ounce; carbonate of ammonia, one-quarter ounce; tincture of cantharides, one-half ounce; mix them well. This mixture will promote the growth of the hair and prevent it from falling out.

Miscellaneous Recipes

EXCELLENT GLYCERINE OINTMENT

A very good preparation of glycerine to have always on hand can be readily prepared by any apothecary or druggist: In two ounces of sweet oil of Almonds melt, by a slow heat, half an ounce of spermaceti, and one drachm of white wax. Then add one ounce of good glycerine, stirring until cold. When cold, scent it by stirring in well a *little* oil of roses. Keep in small jars or small wide-necked bottles. In hot weather keep closely corked, as it sometimes gets a little rancid if long exposed to warmth. Half or a fourth of the above quantities may be used. Every drug store should keep a jar of it and recommend its use. It is excellent for softening the skin; for most injured skin surfaces that are not open sores; for chafed places; for moistening corns or calloused feet or toes; and especially for chapped face, lips, or hands. When the hands are chapped or cracked, or roughened by cold, wash them clean with soap, and rub them well with this glycerine ointment, wiping it off enough to prevent soiling clothing. If this is done at night the hands will be soft and in good condition in the morning, except when deeply cracked. It is very good to apply to the hands after "washing-day." This is an excellent preparation to use by those afflicted with the distressing trouble known as haemorrhoids, or piles.

TO REMOVE WARTS

The best application is said to be that of mono-hydrated nitric acid. The ordinary acid should not be used, because its caustic effects extend much farther than the points touched, while the action of the stronger acid here recommended is limited to the parts to which it is actually applied. Nitrate of silver is also frequently used with advantage, and of late a concentrated soluton of chloral has been spoken of as efficient in destroying warts.

CURE FOR CORNS

Take a well-ripened lemon, roll and squeeze until the juices are well liquified, then open an end of the lemon and squeeze the juice into a glass vial. Add to the juice three or six pearl buttons, according to size, such as are used on linen or cambric underwear. In a few days it will be found the lemon juice has eaten up or dissolved the buttons, so they can be mashed between the thumb and finger. Shake the mixture well, then apply it to the corn. A few applications will conquer the most stubborn settler and give permanent relief. This is a remedy easily prepared, and contains no poisonous substance, so all who desire can use it without fear of evil consequences.

TO CURE BILIOUS HEADACHE

1. Drink the juice of two oranges or of one lemon, about half an hour before breakfast every morning. 2. Dissolve and drink two teaspoonfuls of finely powdered charcoal in half a tumblerful of water; it will relieve in fifteen minutes. Take a Seidlitz powder an hour afterwards.

TO CURE HOARSENESS

Beat well the whites of two eggs, add two tablespoonfuls of white sugar, grate in half a nutmeg, add a pint of luke-warm water, stir well and drink often. Repeat the preparation if necessary.

TREATMENT FOR DIPHTHERIA

One teaspoonful sulphur in a wine-glass of water. Gargle the throat, and swallow a small quantity.

LINIMENT FOR RHEUMATISM

One-half ounce gum camphor, one-half ounce ammonia, one-half ounce sulphuric ether, one-half pint alcohol. Mix together in a bottle; shake before using. To be applied externally; must not be bound on with cloths as it will blister. Does not grease clothing. Can be applied two or three times a day. This has never been known to fail if used regularly.

SENNA PRUNES

Twenty-four prunes, two tablespoons senna leaves, one pint of boiling water. Steep senna in the water where it will keep hot two hours, then strain, wash stew pan, and put in the senna water and prunes. Cover and simmer until the prunes have absorbed all the water, then put in a jar and use as required for constipation. These are delicious and will keep for months.

SPICED BLACKBERRIES

One pound of sugar, one pint of vinegar, one teaspoonful of powdered cinnamon, one teaspoonful of allspice, one teaspoonful of cloves, one teaspoonful of nutmeg. Boil all together gently fifteen minutes, then add four quarts of blackberries, and scald (not boil) ten minutes more. The spice can be omitted if preferred. These are excellent for children in case of summer complaint, and where blackberries are abundant every family should have a plentiful supply.

Dishes for Invalids

CREAM SOUP

One pint boiling water, one-half teacup cream; add broken pieces of toasted bread and a little salt.

EGG GRUEL

Beat the yolk of an egg with one tablespoon sugar, beating the white separately. Add one teacup boiling water to the yolk, then stir in the white, and add any kind of seasoning. Especially good for a cold.

RICE JELLY

Boil a fourth of a pound of rice flour with a half pound of loaf sugar in one quart of water until it becomes one mass; strain off the jell and let it cool.

BEEF TEA

Mince one pound of good lean beef and put into a jar with one teacupful cold water, cork closely and set in a boiler or steamer to cook. It will require three or four hours; strain and season.

ARROWROOT

Use milk or water as preferred; put a heaping teaspoonful ground arrowroot into a cup and mix with a little cold milk. Stir into a pan containing a pint of either cream or water that has been brought to a boil, adding a little salt. Let it simmer a few minutes and then pour out. May be sweetened or flavored with grated nutmeg as desired; should be made only as it is wanted.

BAKED MILK

Put the milk in a jar, covering the opening with white paper, and bake in a moderate oven until thick as cream. May be taken by the most delicate stomach.

A DAINTY SOUP

Boil a small chicken in enough water to cover it; skim and strain when done. Make a mustard of one egg well beaten, a little salt, half a pint of milk; put it in a cup and set in boiling water until it is done. Then with a teaspoon cut out dumplings and drop them into your soup.

PANADA

Put two or three soda crackers into a bowl, pour boiling water over them until they are swelled, sprinkle a little sugar over them, add a cup of boiling water and a tablespoonful of wine, and flavor to taste.

WINE POSSET

In one pint of milk boil two or three slices of bread; when soft, remove from the stove, add a little grated nutmeg and one teaspoon sugar, and then pour into it slowly one-half pint sweet wine. Serve it with toasted bread.

WINE WHEY

One pint sweet milk; boil and pour into it sherry wine until it curdles, then strain and use whey.

CINNAMON TEA

To a half pint fresh new milk, add stick or ground cinnamon enough to flavor and sugar to taste. Bring to boiling point and take either hot or cold. Excellent for diarrhea. Brandy may be added if needed.

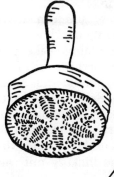

Acknowledgments

T HE COMPILATION of this cookbook would have been impossible without assistance from many others. I am greatly indebted to the staff of the Nebraska State Historical Society, and especially Mrs. Louise Small, Librarian, and Mrs. Opal Jacobsen of the Photograph Collection, who were unstintingly helpful in locating material and providing photos; Professor Bernice Slote, University of Nebraska–Lincoln, on whose wide knowledge of the social history of Willa Cather's Nebraska I have relied heavily; Mr. Barry B. Combs, Director of Public Relations for the Union Pacific Railroad, Omaha, who supplied much information for the railroad chapter; Mrs. Nellie Snyder Yost of North Platte and Mr. George W. LeRoy, Superintendent, Buffalo Bill's Ranch State Historical Park, who assisted with the section on cowboy cookery; the Chicago Corral of Westerners, who permitted the use of the material quoted from Ramon Adams's "Cookie" in *This Is the West*, edited by Robert West Howard, © 1957 by the Chicago Corral of Westerners; Mrs. Francis Jacobs Alberts of Hastings, who gave permission for the use of the recipes for corn cob syrup and Irish potato pie from her compilation *Sod House Memories*; Mrs. Caroline Sandoz Pifer, who furnished Mari Sandoz's recipes and authorized the use of material from her writings; and Mrs. Milton Beechner of Lincoln, who contributed favorite recipes of her mother, Bess Streeter Aldrich. Professor Paolo E. Coletta of Annapolis, Maryland, and Mr. Robert A. Murray of Sheridan, Wyoming, offered valuable leads to information.

Thanks are also due the Nebraskans and former Nebraskans who supplied recipes from their family cookbooks: Mrs. Alice McCulloch of Ogden, Utah, for Dutch apple cake, prune cake, and yellow tomato preserves; Mrs. Robert Dineen of Lincoln for apple strudel, potato dumplings and svitek; Mrs. A. G. Stauffer of Kearney for cheese and soap; Mrs. Sally Dzingle of Loup City for pierogi and prune soup; Mrs. Rose Uzendoski of Fullerton for pigs' feet, czarnina, egg noodles, and cheese cakes; Mrs. Francis Doyle of Red Cloud for sauerkraut; and Mrs. Jennie Miner Reiher of Red Cloud for the hickory nut cake of *My Ántonia*.

I owe a special debt of gratitude to Miss Virginia Faulkner, Editor of the University of Nebraska Press, valued friend and mentor, who was a constant source of encouragement and sound advice, and Mrs. Peggy W. Link, who found time in a busy schedule to furnish the drawings. My mother, Mrs. Alma Hall Graber, assisted in the preparation of the manuscript.

In addition to the titles mentioned above and the works of Mari Sandoz and Willa Cather referred to in the text, a number of books stand out as particularly helpful sources of information. James C. Olson's *History of Nebraska* (Lincoln: University of Nebraska Press, 1955) is a gold mine of general historical background. *Mollie: The Journal of Mollie Dorsey Sanford in Nebraska and Colorado Territories, 1857–1866* (Lincoln: University of Nebraska Press, 1959); Mont Hawthorne's story, *Them Was the Days: An American Saga of the '70's*, by Martha Ferguson McKeown (Lincoln: University of Nebraska Press, 1961); and *Western Story: The Recollections of Charley O'Kieffe, 1884–1898* (Lincoln: University of Nebraska Press, 1960) offer a vivid first-hand picture of how Nebraska's early settlers lived; and *The Sod House Frontier, 1854–1890*, by Everett Dick (Lincoln: Johnsen Publishing Co., 1954) is a rich source of social history of the homestead period in general. *Pinnacle Jake*, by A. B. Snyder and Nellie Snyder Yost (Lincoln: University of Nebraska Press, 1962) gives an authentic view of the cowboy's life. Robert G. Athearn's *Westward the*

Briton (Lincoln: University of Nebraska Press, 1962) and Sir Richard Burton's *The Look of the West, 1860* (Lincoln: University of Nebraska Press, 1963) contain much interesting material on British travelers in the American West, while the Mormon emigration is recorded in *Among the Mormons: Historic Accounts by Contemporary Observers*, edited by William Mulder and A. Russell Mortensen (Lincoln: University of Nebraska Press, 1973). Kate McPhelim Cleary's articles are reprinted in *The Nebraska of Kate McPhelim Cleary* (Lake Bluff, Ill.: United Educators, Inc., 1958). Two handwritten notebooks donated to the Nebraska State Historical Society by Miss Ruth Sheldon, along with a number of locally produced cookbooks from Nebraska towns, were especially useful examples of recipe collections dating from the state's pioneer period.

All of the photographs are from the collection of the Nebraska State Historical Society.

KAY GRABER

Acknowledgments   157

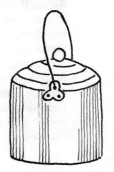

Index

Index

Index